Low-Risk Strategies

Low-Risk Strategies

For the High-Performance Investor

Thomas C. Noddings

PROBUS PUBLISHING COMPANY • Chicago, IL 60606

Library of Congress Cataloging in Publication Data

Noddings, Thomas C.
Low-risk strategies for the high-performance investor.

Includes index.
1. Convertible bonds. I. Title.
HG4651.N63 1985 332.63'23 84–26223
ISBN 0-917253-09-4

Library of Congress Catalog Card No. 84–26223

Printed in the United States of America

1 2 3 4 5 6 7 8 9 0

To my wife,
FRAN
for all her patience and caring
through the years

Contents

Foreword

When Thomas Noddings decided to write this book for the smaller investor, I applauded. As an investment broker working principally with high-net-worth, tax-fretting investors, I am continually amazed at how even the wealthy rarely look beyond stocks, bonds, and money market instruments in their quest for capital growth.

One of the most often overlooked investment areas is convertible securities—especially convertible bonds. I've found that investors either haven't taken the time to understand "converts," as they are called, or they rarely encounter a specialist who can authoritatively advise them on the subject. Indeed, they cannot find a suitable explanation of the basics. I know. I have looked.

The best way to explain convertible securities to the novice is to compare them to automobiles. Convertibles, of course, are back in fashion. They are rolling off the assembly lines in Detroit and Japan after years of being shelved. Convertible securities are finally getting the spotlight. While they have always been in vogue with institutional and sophisticated investors, Main Street is now taking a cue from Wall Street.

Convertibles offer you a choice. A convertible automobile lets you enjoy the excitement of the open road with the wind in your hair, yet it can also protect you against the cold and the rain. Convertible bonds provide stock market opportunity but combine it with the security of the bond market as well. If stocks climb, you can convert your bonds into common shares and cash in on the appreciation. If interest rates rise and the stock market falls, you hold onto your bonds, since you have downside protection and collect interest income while waiting for the next market upturn.

Mr. Noddings is not just an expert authority on what many might feel is an arcane subject. He is an "educator" who has a sound performance record. It is precisely these two factors that make this book fascinating for the smaller, serious, first-time convertible investor.

The juncture where Mr. Noddings departs from other investment specialists—specialists who write books or lecture extensively—is a crucial point. Most authors or speakers on the circuit see their publishing or lecturing as a prime source of compensation or ego gratification; their investment practice takes a back seat to the lecturn. Although Mr. Noddings has written five considerably detailed texts on convertible securities for the investment technician and always shared his strategies for success, he has never diverted his attention away from the mandate of his profession: The achievement of capital appreciation for his clientele, a goal tailored to their individual risk acceptance level.

He has been a pioneer in designing strategies which allow investors to choose an investment comfort level that is compatible with their personal investment goals. As an investment broker with a keen knowledge of the competition, I have not encountered another investment professional who has been able to both separate the risk component into segments that appeal to a spectrum of the investing community and to deliver maximum yields or rewards for each segment. Tom Noddings has achieved that seemingly impossible task.

Mr. Noddings uses a number of different strategies for his clients. One is termed "Low-Risk Convertibles," which uses converts where the underlying stocks are rated B+ or better according to Standard & Poor's. Since 1975, his firm's low-risk convertible bond index has produced a cumulative gain of 282 percent, compared to 157 percent for the higher risk Standard & Poor's 500 Stock Index and 57 percent for blue chip corporate bonds.

Another strategy for the investor who is willing to assume more risk in the hope of realizing greater rewards involves convertible securities with underlying stocks of generally secondary quality and, therefore, higher volatility. While riskier, this approach offers greater profit potential; his firm's index of "Aggressive Convertibles" has posted a cumulative gain of 438 percent over the same 8½ year period.

Mr. Noddings has culled nearly 20 years of experience exclusively with convertible securities to perfect "high-performance/low-risk" investing. In my estimation, it is destined to alter investor views on the conventional risk/reward ratio. Step by step he explains how the volatility of the stock market can be tempered if not tamed by the smaller investor.

This visionary concept of understanding and managing investment risk should break new ground in other areas of investing, I believe. Mr. Noddings has shown that the fundamentalist and the technician do not have to live in two different worlds but can co-exist harmoniously when the investor's needs and goals are the top priority.

Mr. Noddings has spent a career putting the investor first. This new book will broaden the scope of his influence and, for the first time, the smaller investor will be a direct beneficiary of his knowledge and insights.

JAY GOLDINGER

Preface

Building and preserving wealth is a perilous business. Follow Wall Street's typical run-of-the-mill advice, and you are destined to watch others achieve your goals. You cannot run with the herd and come out a winner! Superior alternatives to conventional investment wisdom do exist, but few investors are aware of them, and fewer use them successfully.

This book will introduce you to a high-performance/low-risk investing program, using overlooked alternatives to traditional stocks, bonds, and money market instruments. When I speak of high performance, doubling your money in a year or two is not what I have in mind. Significant participation in stock market advances, at much less risk during declines, truly defines high performance for me. Over time, a low-risk strategy of this nature will actually provide greater profits than the higher-risk stock market. Patient investors will be abundantly rewarded.

Individuals *can* achieve high, *total-portfolio performance* without incurring stock-market-type risk through the use of the strategies presented in this book. Let me stress that these strategies do not call for special market insights or a crystal ball. They do require that you accept the fact that inefficiencies do exist in certain market sectors. You, as an individual investor, can exploit these inefficiencies to your advantage.

Undervalued convertible bonds are the key to low-risk/high-performance investing. Carefully selected convertibles can give you fixed-income safety while providing stock market opportunity. Purchased by institutional money managers on the new-issue offerings, convertible bonds are largely avoided by the institutions in the trading aftermarket. It is here, in the aftermarket, that smaller investors can find incredible bargains. This book will show you how to analyze these opportunities and exploit them.

The fact that IBM, the bluest of the blue chips, uses convertibles casts aside the widely held misconception that convertible bonds are only issued by speculative companies. To finance its recent acquisition of Rolm Corporation, IBM announced a new convertible bond having a market value exceeding $1 billion (the largest convertible issue ever). A sister "blue chip," AT&T, has also used convertible securities to raise capital, as have numerous other Fortune 500 companies.

I urge those unfamiliar with convertibles to read this book in its entirety without stopping to ponder the terms and concepts you may be encountering for the first time. A quick once through will give you a more solid foundation for digesting the subject matter on a second reading. During your second reading, ask questions as you go along—questions that you must try to answer by yourself. This analytical learning approach is preeminently necessary for the sake of comprehension and enlightenment.

In preparing this book I have been aided greatly by many friends and associates. Chief among them was Earl Zazove of E. Zazove and Associates, a Chicago-based investment advisory firm. Dr. Zazove is a nationally recognized expert in the field of convertible securities. I sincerely appreciate his invaluable contributions in making this a definitive work.

Special thanks to my assistant, Consuelo Castanuela. Without Connie's initiative and analysis this book would not exist.

THOMAS C. NODDINGS

CHAPTER 1

The Risks and Rewards of Investment

There are many kinds of investors. At one extreme we find those having confidence in the future, knowing their money is growing steadily and surely. Others, at the opposite end of the spectrum, are full of anxiety, their sleep ruined by uncertainty.

These diametrically positioned investors may wind up enjoying the same results over the long term, but *which investor would you rather be?* Consider two alternative five-year investment programs:

	Annual Returns	
Year	*Investor A*	*Investor B*
1	+10%	+20%
2	+ 9	−10
3	+12	+30
4	+ 8	−15
5	+11	+35

Investor A has a low-risk investment approach, perhaps a money market fund. Relatively stable rates of return fluctuate between 8 and 12 percent; he is happy, relaxed, and confident. Investor B's portfolio offers high returns in some years—as much as 35 percent—but it is also risky. Its value can decline, giving him annual losses of up to 15 percent. His volatile investments may be in the stock market. Would you rather be Investor A or Investor B?

Your answer cannot depend on profits alone, for both investors realized the same 61 percent total appreciation over the five years—a 10 percent compounded (annualized) rate of return.[1] Rather, with this example, your answer must depend on whether you prefer stability or uncertainty, calm or anxiety. The two programs vary considerably in their volatility or risk, and so do the investors' blood pressures.

People differ greatly in how much risk they like in their lives. Some enjoy NASCAR racing, hang gliding, and volatile investments. Treasuring excitement, they might well be bored by Investor A's passive approach. Others preferring quieter lives would find Investor B's aggressive strategy far too nerve-wracking. Which kind of person are you?

Whatever your answer to this question, bear in mind that successful investing always involves trade-offs between risk and reward. If you enjoy or can stand high risk, you can look forward to the prospect of high rewards. If you refuse all possible risk, you must be content with lesser rewards. Whatever your choice, your objective should always be to earn the highest return available for the level of risk you assume. You want your risk to be fairly rewarded by future returns.

The trouble is, few investment strategies are entirely predictable. Rates of return will vary from year to year, and a run of bad luck is always a possibility, although bad and good years do tend to average out over the long haul. While short-term investors are rightly leery of volatile investments, truly long-term investors see less risk even in programs whose returns fluctuate wildly from year to year.

In addition, all profits are reduced by such factors as income taxes, management fees, and brokerage commissions. We can see the effect of the first of these expenses by looking again at our two investors. Let's assume that all the appreciation earned by Investor B were taxed at the lower rate for long-term capital gains. Even if this investor was in a modest income tax bracket, his after-tax return would be higher than if he had earned fully taxable income each year like Investor A. Therefore, Investor B's volatile, high-risk strategy might be appropriate for many individuals if favorable tax consequences are important. This assumes, however, that such aggressive investors have the temperament to ride out the down moves of a market cycle, without losing their nerve and selling out near the bottom. They must regard investing as a *long-term* proposition.

On the other hand, an investor seeking a strategy for his company's tax-sheltered pension or profit-sharing plan, or for his Individual Retirement Account (IRA), would probably opt for the lower-risk approach used by Investor A. Why incur the sleepless nights associated with volatile markets if there are no advantages to be gained?

Inflation is another critical variable in the risk-reward equation. Most investors know what inflation means in a general sense, but they may have difficulty relating it to their personal investment decisions. True investments, according to most definitions (including mine), must have the potential to enhance purchasing power or wealth. Thus, the *real* return for any investment strategy is the after-tax earnings minus the rate of inflation. If Investors A and B were both taxed at the maximum rates on their 10 percent annualized returns, their net results in an inflation-free environment would be quite satisfactory. However, if inflation was running at 10 percent, as it has in recent times, both would be losers. Investor B, for example, would lose an inflation-adjusted 2 percent if taxed at the 20 percent maximum for long-term capital gains (8 percent after-tax minus 10 percent inflation). Investor A would suffer a real return of −5 percent per year if taxed at the 50 percent maximum for income received (5 percent after-tax minus 10 percent inflation). Suddenly, a "risk-free" 10 percent return becomes a devastating loss of purchasing power, hardly a winning proposition. As I will demonstrate shortly, traditional risk-free and low-risk investments have destroyed more wealth in recent years than the great stock market crash of 1929.

HIGH-RETURN INVESTING

I said that high risk goes with high reward, yet I gave Investors A and B the same 10 percent compounded rate of return despite the large differences in their risks. This allowed me to simplify the illustrations, especially the tax impact on individual investors. However, what happens under more realistic conditions? The following table introduces Investor C to our discussion by assuming 5 percent higher yearly returns (or lower losses) than experienced by Investor B. Now, *which investor would you rather be?*

	Annual Returns		
Year	*Investor A*	*Investor B*	*Investor C*
1	+10%	+20%	+ 25%
2	+ 9	−10	− 5
3	+12	+30	+ 35
4	+ 8	−15	− 10
5	+11	+35	+ 40
Five-year appreciation:	+61%	+61%	+102%
Annualized return:	+10%	+10%	+ 15%

Investor C doubled his money over the five year period via a 15 percent compounded rate of return. His annual returns fluctuated just as widely as Investor B's, but he dropped less in bad years and gained more in good years. His strategy clearly improved the relationship between risk and reward. If his returns were taxed as long-term capital gains, he would enjoy net profits even in the face of 10 percent inflation.

Most tax-paying investors should surely prefer this high-return strategy to the "comfort" of a money market fund. In fact, even as a trustee for tax-sheltered pension and profit-sharing plans, I would select Investor C's approach over Investor A's without hesitation. In my opinion, the wealth-building opportunities afforded by high-return investing far overshadow the supposed "safety" of risk-free money market instruments.

However, Investor C's approach is not the best of all possible strategies; it still involves a high degree of risk, as one might experience in the stock market. The purpose of my book is to show you how to realize above average returns while significantly reducing risk. The key is an investment instrument that allows you to construct a conservative portfolio while still giving you stock market opportunity. This low-risk/high-performance instrument is the *convertible bond.* I will begin to discuss convertible bonds in Chapter 2. For now, let's examine the historical risk-reward characteristics of *traditional* investments: common stocks, bonds, and money market instruments.

TRADITIONAL INVESTING

Most investors view risk as the possibility of losing money over a relatively short period, such as a year. They see reward as the possibility of making money over that same period. Other investors take a more relative view, calling "reward" only what they can get *above* the going rate for risk-free money. Thus, if money market funds were yielding 10 percent, Investor C's return range of −10 percent to +40 percent would become 20 percent below and 30 percent above the 10 percent benchmark, a high-risk/high-return strategy by almost anyone's definition. These performance swings from year to year are typical of the blue chip sector of the stock market. (Other investment arenas, such as secondary common stocks and commodity programs, are even more volatile.)

Market scholars have given us a more precise analysis of risk and reward by studying long-term historical rates of return and their variability. In their book, *Stocks, Bonds, Bills and Inflation: The Past and the Future,*[2] Roger Ibbotson and Rex Sinquefield analyzed a compilation of historical data developed by the Center for Research in Security Prices at the University of Chicago. Table 1–1 presents 1926–81 data from the book, updated using other sources through 1983. The performance data shows total annualized returns; they include capital gains plus dividend or interest income, but exclude portfolio management expenses and taxes.

The table compares rates of return for stocks, bonds, and U.S. government Treasury bills, with inflation as measured by the Consumer Price Index (CPI). The common stock proxy is Standard & Poor's (S&P) Composite Stock Index. The authors used the S&P Index because they consid-

Table 1–1. Annual compounded rates of return for traditional investments

	58 Years 1926–83	*10 Years 1974–83*	*5 Years 1979–83*
Consumer price index	+3.0%	+ 8.2%	+ 8.4%
Treasury bills*	+3.2	+ 8.7	+11.1
Corporate bonds†	+4.2	+ 6.4	+ 6.8
Common stocks‡	+9.6	+10.5	+17.3
Tax-exempt bonds§	—	+ 2.7	+ 2.4

* Bank certificates of deposit and other cash substitutes may be considered alternatives to Treasury bills.

† Salomon Brothers High Grade Long-Term Corporate Bond Index.

‡ Standard & Poor's Composite Stock Index.

§ Standard & Poor's Municipal Bond Index.

Source: Roger G. Ibbotson and Rex A. Sinquefield, *Stocks, Bonds, Bills and Inflation: The Past and the Future,* 1982 ed. (Charlottesville, Va.: The Financial Analysis Research Foundation, 1982.) Data updated by other sources through 1983.

ered it a carefully constructed, market-value-weighted measure of common stock performance. "Market-value-weighted" means that the emphasis given to each stock in the index is proportional to its price times the number of shares outstanding. Also referred to as the S&P 500, the index currently includes 500 of the largest companies in the United States; prior to 1957, it was based on 90 companies.

The data presented in Table 1–1, and the detailed support material provided by Ibbotson and Sinquefield in their book, allows us to evaluate the risk-reward characteristics for traditional investments. These instruments comprise the bulk of our nation's capital markets. Thus, their historical performance data should be reasonably good indicators of past pre-expense results achieved by both individual investors and professional money managers. A knowledge of these risk-reward relationships will help you to plan for the future, and to evaluate the low-risk/high-performance strategies I will present later.

Treasury Bills

Treasury bills, issued in 3- to 12-month maturities, provide a riskless benchmark against which other, higher-risk investments may be compared. Contrary to a popular belief within the financial community, risk-free instruments have not provided real (inflation-adjusted) returns of 3 to 4 percent. As shown in Table 1–1, T-bill returns of 3.2 percent, over the long term, have only slightly exceeded the 3.0 percent inflation rate. During the 30s and 40s, T-bill interest was typically less than one percent. When inflation heated up in the late 60s, T-bill rates rose in parallel. They reached their peak, at more than 14 percent in 1981, following two consecutive years of double-digit inflation. Since 1981, T-bills have provided a modest real return—the first time since the Great Depression. Deflation during the 30s turned low interest rates into high *real* returns.

According to our definition, true investments must have the ability to build wealth. Risk-free instruments like T-bills or bank certificates of deposit should keep pace with inflation in tax-deferred trusts such as an IRA account, but they will probably not add to wealth in the future any more than they have in the past. Banks and others who advertise that a $2,000 annual contribution to an IRA account will grow to a million dollars by retirement are seriously misleading the investment public. The IRA's *nominal* value may grow to a million (or more) expressed in terms of dollars, but not in purchasing power. For a $2,000 annual investment to be truly worth $1,000,000 after 40 years, a real return of 10 percent per year is imperative.

In an inflationary environment, "risk-free investing" by people who pay taxes is a virtual guarantee that their wealth will be destroyed over time. As a tax-paying investor, would you rather earn 1.0 percent pre-tax with zero inflation, or 10 percent when inflation is running at 9 percent? Both provide a pre-tax 1.0 percent inflation-adjusted return. However, assuming a 30 percent tax bracket, the *after-tax real rates of return* are +0.7 percent for the first choice and −2.0 percent for the second. At a 50 percent tax rate, the after-tax numbers are +0.5 and −4.0 percent. How many of today's retired people are living off unusually high interest rates earned on their money market funds, not realizing that they are spending their own capital and not real earnings?

Inflation, the primary cause of high interest rates, is really a retrogressive tax on the most productive sector of our society, our nation's savers. This is an extremely serious situation. Our country's growth and prosperity depend on millions of small savers, many of whom are still earning below-market rates of return from passbook savings and checking accounts.

U.S. Government and Corporate Bonds

Long-term government and corporate bonds, maturing in 20–30 years, have traditionally been considered the financial anchor for most professionally managed portfolios. In a stock and bond portfolio, bonds are intended to stabilize the principal while stocks provide the asset growth.

Unfortunately, as inflation accelerated, driving interest rates skyward, bond prices adjusted to the high-interest environment by declining precipitously. The 4.2 percent earned from corporate bonds over 58 years, 1926–83, exceeded inflation by only 1.2 percent (see Table 1–1). In recent years, bonds have actually failed to match inflation, despite 1982, when they rallied by 44 percent. This was their largest one-year total return in the entire 58-year period. The next best year was 1976, with an 18.6 percent return.

The prevailing wisdom after the great stock market crash was that sound investing meant only bonds; common stocks were considered far too speculative. This ill-timed thinking ushered in the great bear market for bonds. It began in 1941 and continued unabated for 40 years. Only time will tell if the huge rally in 1982 has broken the 40-year downtrend.

The worst five-year period in the bond market's history was 1977–81. On a pre-tax, inflation-adjusted basis, the five-year total returns obtainable from long-term government and corporates were each −42 percent. This compares with −28 percent for the poorest five-year period in the stock market, 1929–33. (Deflation in the early 30s protected the purchasing power of stock market investments to some extent, since actual total returns for S&P stocks fell by 45 percent between 1929 and 1933.)

Most people, I believe, are largely unaware that inflation has destroyed the wealth of those investors holding long-term, fixed-income securities. Since the equity for the typical household in this country is primarily a personal residence, homeowners have been largely sheltered from inflation's ravages. Most people seem to enjoy watching their home values rise year after year, being unaware (or not caring) that mortgages are made possible by savers who are suffering the consequences of "prudent investing."

Herbert Stein, chairman of the Council of Economic Advisors under Presidents Nixon and Ford, described a related effect of inflation in the March 30, 1984 issue of the *Wall Street Journal:*

> In 1946, after the end of World War II, the federal debt was $242 billion. Since then, Washington has run a total budget deficit of nearly $800 billion. But the federal debt today, in 1946 prices, is $232 billion. The real value of the debt is smaller today, despite the cumulative deficit. This magic has been performed by inflation. We have gradually but effectively repudiated all of the postwar debt by inflation. How effective this repudiation has been can be seen from the following example: Suppose a person had bought a 20-year Treasury bond in 1944 for $1,000. In 1964 he reinvests the $1,000 at maturity in another Treasury bond. This year he finally collects his $1,000. It is now worth $200. During this period the investor received interest, first at the rate of 2.5 percent and then, after 1964, at the rate of 4.2 percent. If we adjust the interest also for

> inflation, we find that his real rate of return on the initial investment was minus 1.2 percent per annum.

Mr. Stein could have taken a big step further by considering federal income taxes paid on the interest earned. The real return would then have been even worse than −1.2 percent. Note his statement that the federal debt was repudiated by inflation. Contrary to popular belief, our huge government deficits are not passed on to future generations. They are paid by our nation's savers through the wealth-destroying process of inflation.

In 1981, Congress passed legislation indexing wages to inflation. While they lowered the maximum rate on "unearned income" (investment income) from 70 percent to 50 percent, no action was taken to protect investment income from rising inflation. Perhaps Congress did not wish to open Pandora's box by admitting that *their* term "unearned income" really means what it says. Income is not income when inflation turns it into a loss, and paying taxes on such illusory earnings is the equivalent of a highly discriminatory national tax on personal property. But how many people are aware of this?

In recent years of high inflation and declining bond prices, tax-paying investors have been hit doubly hard. Not only did pre-tax bond returns underperform inflation, but investors were required to pay taxes on the extraordinarily high interest received while not being allowed to offset the interest earned by their bond losses.

One would hope that Congress would eventually correct the past wrongs inflicted on beleaguered fixed-income investors. Alas, the so-called "tax reform" act of 1984 poured salt on their wounds. Buyers of newly issued bonds, purchased at a discount, must now treat future price appreciation as income rather than capital gains. Thus, future bondholders will experience even greater price declines during periods of rising interest rates, since buyers will insist on lower prices to offset the adverse tax consequences.

Tax-Exempt Bonds

During interviews with prospective clients, I am always questioned about the performance of my managed accounts; the past year and the past five years are the time frames that most concern investors. I welcome these questions, especially about long-term performance, yet I suspect that the vast majority of investors fail to ask similar questions when faced by salesmen promoting tax-free investments.

For example, during the past decade, tax-exempt municipal bond trusts have been one of the easiest sales for stockbrokers to make to their conservative, income-oriented clients. Who doesn't want tax-free income? How many investors have not reached the 35 percent tax bracket, the approximate level at which tax-free interest is more advantageous than the higher interest earned on fully taxable bonds? But how often do tax-exempt buyers check to see how these same instruments did in the past? Let's examine the record.

For the ten years from 1974 to 1983, high-quality tax-exempts returned only 2.7 percent annually (see Table 1–1). With the CPI at 8.2 percent over that period, wealth was destroyed at a rate exceeding 5 percent per year. This assumes that all tax-free interest ranging from 5 to 10 percent was reinvested. Those who spent the income saw their wealth plummet by more than 10 percent annually!

As with long-term government and corporate bonds, municipals have been unable to escape the inflationary storm. Inflation and plummeting prices more than offset the deceptively high interest rates, leaving bondholders with negative real returns to show for their "conservatively" invested dollars. In addition, adding insult to injury, the widely perceived safety of tax-exempts was seriously challenged by the New York City and Washington Public Power Supply System debacles. The net result was that municipal bonds, so-called tax loopholes for the rich, have destroyed wealth in this nation to an unprecedented extent. If investors were aware of these shocking results, they might think twice about this "sure-thing" investment and continue their search for better after-tax alternatives.

Common Stocks

Common stocks were the only investment alternative that clearly beat the Consumer Price Index, by an annualized 9.6 percent return versus 3.0 percent, over the 58 years of Table 1–1. However, as we might expect, the year-to-year results were highly variable.

The largest single-year loss was 43.3 percent in 1931; the largest gain was 54.0 percent just two years later, in 1933. More recently, the S&P index dropped 26.5 percent in 1974, but immediately, in 1975, rallied with a 37.2 percent gain. These were the largest single-year changes in the last twenty years.

Common stocks are clearly less risky in the longer term. The lowest ten-year annualized return was −0.9 percent from 1929 to 1938, while the highest was 20.1 percent from 1949 to 1958. These figures, however, do not reflect changes in wealth, since they do not account for inflation. On an inflation-adjusted basis, the greatest 10-year annualized loss, occurring quite recently, exceeded that of the Great Depression. It was −3.4 percent between 1969 and 1978. The highest return was 17.9 percent, from 1949–58, the same best ten-year period as above. Taking longer time spans into account, we see no losing twenty-year periods for common stocks either before or after adjusting for inflaion. Common stocks are clearly the *only* investment that outperformed inflation over the long term as well as during the recent years following the 1974 bear market.

CREATING WEALTH

There is a magic to compounding high rates of return over very long periods of time. Consider an investor who, in 1926, had $1,000 to invest. By 1983, if he had put his money in Treasury bills, he would have $6,300. If he had put it in corporate bonds, he would have $10,900. If he had put it in common stocks (the S&P Composite Stock Index), he would have $199,000. His third option would have paid off 20–30 times better than the first two. Taxes would lower the final figures, but common stocks would then show even greater advantages over T-bills and bonds since much of the stock market's appreciation was in the form of lower-taxed capital gains.

I cannot overemphasize that risks associated with most investment programs are significantly reduced as time passes. The longer the time span, the higher the probability that one's investment objective will be met. Real estate investors understand this principle well, but many stock market "investors" seek instant gratification and quickly become discouraged if their selections don't pay immediate profits. I must also emphasize again that risk and reward *must* be related to the preservation of purchas-

Table 1–2. Potential appreciation over time for $1,000 invested today

Annual Return	*Final Value*			
	5 Years	*10 Years*	*20 Years*	*40 Years*
5%	$1,300	$1,600	$ 2,600	$ 7,000
10	1,600	2,600	6,700	45,000
15	2,000	4,000	16,000	270,000
20	2,500	6,200	38,000	1,500,000

ing power in inflationary times, a goal that most investors have found to be highly elusive.

Table 1–2 provides capital appreciation numbers for rates of return ranging from 5 to 20 percent and over periods of 5 to 40 years. This table clearly demonstrates that high-performance investing is worth the extra time and effort needed to search out superior opportunities such as those I will present in the next chapters. This is how fortunes are built and future retirement income secured.

NOTES FOR CHAPTER

1. *Total return* for any investment program over more than one time period is determined by linking performance data for the individual periods. For the two examples, their returns for each of the five years are linked as follows:

$$\text{Investor A: } 1.10 \times 1.09 \times 1.12 \times 1.08 \times 1.11 = 1.61$$
$$\text{Investor B: } 1.20 \times 0.90 \times 1.30 \times 0.85 \times 1.35 = 1.61$$

A *linked index* of 1.61 means a 61 percent total return. The *annualized* return can be determined from the following equation.

$$R = \sqrt[N]{(1 + R_1)\ (1 + R_2)\ (1 + R_3) \cdots (1 + R_N)} - 1$$

For Investor B, the annualized return is computed as follows:

$$\begin{aligned} R &= \sqrt[5]{(1.20)\ (0.90)\ (1.30)\ (0.85)\ (1.35)} - 1 \\ &= \sqrt[5]{1.61} - 1 \\ &= 1.10 - 1 \text{ or } 10\% \end{aligned}$$

The resulting 10 percent return is called the geometric mean. More commonly it is referred to as the compounded annual rate of return or for further simplification, the annualized return or annualized rate of return.

2. Roger G. Ibbotson and Rex A. Sinquefield, *Stocks, Bonds, Bills and Inflation: The Past and the Future* 1982 ed. (Charlottesville, Va.: The Financial Analysts Research Foundation, 1982.)

CHAPTER 2

The Investment Decision

I hope Chapter 1 convinced you that common stocks are a better long-term investment than money market or fixed-income securities. Stocks have historically offered much higher long-term yields; however, they *are* volatile.

Few investors have the psychological stamina to withstand the exposure of all their capital to the stock market's volatility, even in broadly diversified portfolios of blue-chip companies. Most investors buy a mix of different types of securities, and the mix can vary. Some go heavy on riskless money market instruments. Others may favor stocks of highly speculative companies.

How do investors decide on their investment mixes? The answer to this question depends very much on how people balance risk and reward. It also leads into several related questions:

- What is the risk-reward posture for an investor's overall program?
- How can investors tell whether they are achieving their investment objectives?
- How can investors tell whether they are performing above or below competitive rates of return, as measured by market standards such as U.S. Treasury bill rates and Standard & Poor's 500 Stock Index?
- When should investors fire their money managers (or fire themselves and seek professional management)?
- Is there a way to relate risk to reward for the purpose of making investment decisions that is easy to understand?

THE CAPITAL MARKET LINE

There *is* a relatively simple way to relate risk to reward. The investment community uses the *capital market line* to portray long-term risk-reward relationships for different investment strategies. It graphically depicts the performance data shown in Table 1–1. Plotting these data as in Exhibit 2–1 gives us a straight-line graph comparing returns for various investment alternatives for the 58 years from 1926 to 1983.

The vertical axis in Exhibit 2–1 represents annualized returns. The horizontal axis indicates risk (relative volatility). Notice that the capital market line intersects the vertical axis at the zero risk level, represented by Treasury bills. As risk is increased, expected return also increases. The solid line's upper region represents a diversified portfolio of good-quality common stocks, such as Standard & Poor's 500 Stock Index or the Dow Jones Industrial Average. The S&P 500, by definition, has a risk level of 1.0.

Exhibit 2–1. The capital market line (58-year data, 1926–83)

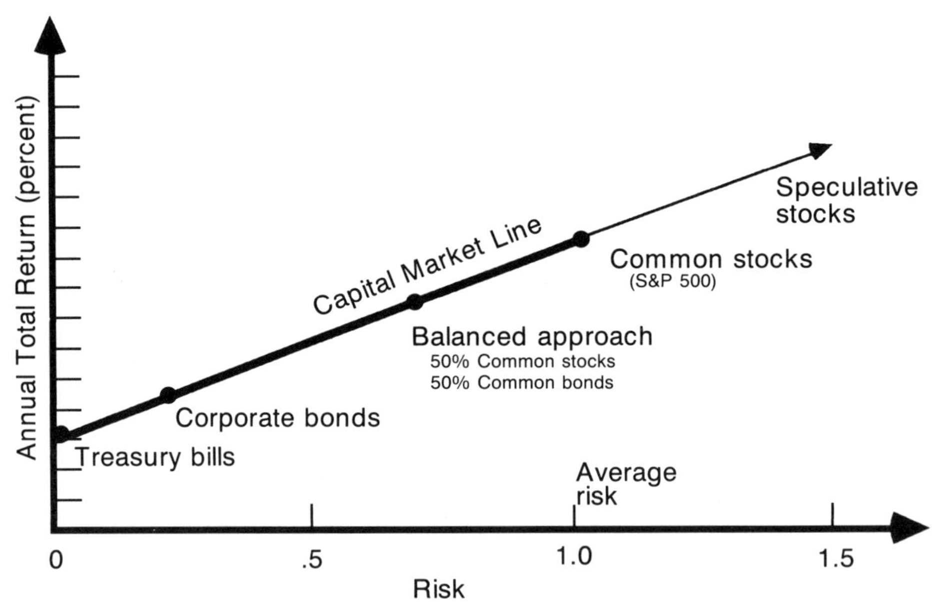

Let me stress that the risk level of a diversified index, such as the S&P 500, is much lower than the risk levels of the individual stocks included in the index. It is even less risky than blue chips, such as General Motors or IBM. Most portfolios owned by individual investors contain but a handful of different stocks. Such nondiversified portfolios experience much higher price volatility than does an index.

The capital market line's dashed extension indicates regions of high risk, such as common stocks of speculative companies. Many speculative stocks are traded on the New York Stock Exchange; most are traded on the American Stock Exchange and the Over-the-Counter Market.

I must emphasize that the capital market line illustrates very long-term relationships. Returns will seldom fall neatly on the straight line over short periods of time. They may not even fall near it. In recent years, long-term bonds, for example, have exhibited greater price volatility than common stocks. Yet bonds provided significantly lower returns. This recent below-the-line performance for bonds contrasts with money market instruments, which have been providing real rates of return (above-the-line performance) for the past few years, the first time since the 30s.

The balanced approach to investing, shown near the center of the capital market line, is typical of professionally managed portfolios for large pension funds and other tax-exempt trusts. These portfolios generally consist of some combination of common stocks and long-term corporate or government bonds. Although an equal mix is illustrated, and by definition is termed the *balanced approach,* most money managers will vary the precise combination based upon their view of the future outlook for each of the two investment strategies. Smaller investors often use short-term money market instruments to balance their stock portfolios.

The capital market line shows only pre-tax performance. Thus, it is most useful when applied to tax-exempt trusts. For tax-paying investors, (individuals or corporations) adjustments must be made. Individuals, for example, will usually purchase lower-yielding municipals instead of taxable bonds. Corporations will often buy preferred stocks because they receive an 85 percent exclusion from taxes on the dividends. Their tax-motivated purchases tend to raise preferred stock price levels above those of bonds even though bonds are safer. Individuals should seldom own preferreds, since they can attain higher yields from inherently less risky bonds.

When someone touts an investment strategy as one that will increase return while reducing risk, ask why and how the strategy is supposed to fall *above* the capital market line. There must be a logical answer! Above-the-line performance is everyone's goal, but it is a goal that is extremely difficult to attain after deducting management fees and brokerage commissions. Professional equity managers, for instance, attempt to outperform the market by selecting stocks which they believe to be undervalued. Yet most have found it to be virtually impossible to beat the S&P 500 without incurring higher risks. Professional fixed-income managers also play the performance game by trying to outguess the interest rate cycle. They jump back and forth between short-term and long-term bonds with no greater success than the stock pickers. The few equity or fixed-income pros who succeed (whether from skill or luck) are generously rewarded by accolades from the financial media. This attention spawns a rush of new clients chasing the latest "hot-hand" managers.

Having said how difficult it is to beat the markets, let's now preview the strategies you will learn about in this book. These are *superior* strategies that have consistently demonstrated their ability to enhance long-term performance, at reduced levels of risk, without depending on a crystal ball. They include a variety of techniques exploiting overlooked niches in today's capital markets, niches that offer attractive risk-reward opportunities to smaller, non-institutional investors.

SUPERIOR INVESTMENT ALTERNATIVES

Practically speaking, the only superior alternatives to traditional investing are those that *cannot* accommodate large institutional portfolios managed by banks, insurance companies, and investment advisors. These professional money managers certainly have the resources to analyze the strategies you are about to learn and to take advantage of undervalued opportunities. However, it is not worth their time and effort if they can't invest large amounts. This book will explore those of our nation's financial market niches avoided by the big institutional money managers. These niches include convertible securities and related instruments for adjusting risk-reward relationships.

Convertible bonds and convertible preferred stocks are hybrid securities that should be viewed as an alternative to a combination of common stocks and straight (nonconvertible) bonds or preferreds. Like a straight bond, a convertible bond provides guaranteed interest (coupon) and a maturity date when the issuing company must redeem it at full par value (usually $1,000). In addition, the issuing company makes a third promise: At the bondholder's option, anytime during the life of the instrument, the company will exchange (convert) it for a stated number of common stock shares. Thus, a convertible bond will both participate in future price advances by its underlying common stock and provide the benefits of fixed income and safety. It is not unusual to find convertible bonds trading up to 100 percent above par and even higher since there is no price ceiling. Convertible preferreds have similar characteristics, except they do not usually have redemption dates.

Many companies, from blue chip to rankly speculative outfits, use convertible bonds to raise capital. Like investors who purchase convertibles, companies consider them as an alternative to issuing conventional stock or bond securities. Once issued, a convertible bond's price will rise or fall in the trading aftermarket along with price changes in its underlying common stock, interest rate changes, and other market variables.

Bought by institutional investors when newly issued, convertibles are largely ignored in the aftermarket since they do not provide the trading liquidity required by large institutional money managers. It is here, in the aftermarket, that smaller investors can gain a substantial edge by carefully monitoring price movements. As I will show in later chapters, undervalued convertibles are *always* available for the smaller investor.

THE CONVERTIBLE STRATEGIES LINE

New convertible bonds at par can generally be considered an alternative to the balanced approach. As their prices advance above par in the future, they take on more of the risk-reward characteristics of common stock. If their prices decline below par they become more like straight bonds. At all times, however, convertibles retain hybrid characteristics relating them to both stocks and bonds.

Since the aftermarket offers convertibles having varying levels of quality and priced from well below par (deep-discounted bonds) to well above par, portfolios can be designed for any risk level an investor wishes to assume. This portfolio management flexibility is illustrated by the *convertible strategies line,* the upper line in Exhibit 2–2, which compares convertible

Exhibit 2–2. The convertible strategies line compared to the capital market line

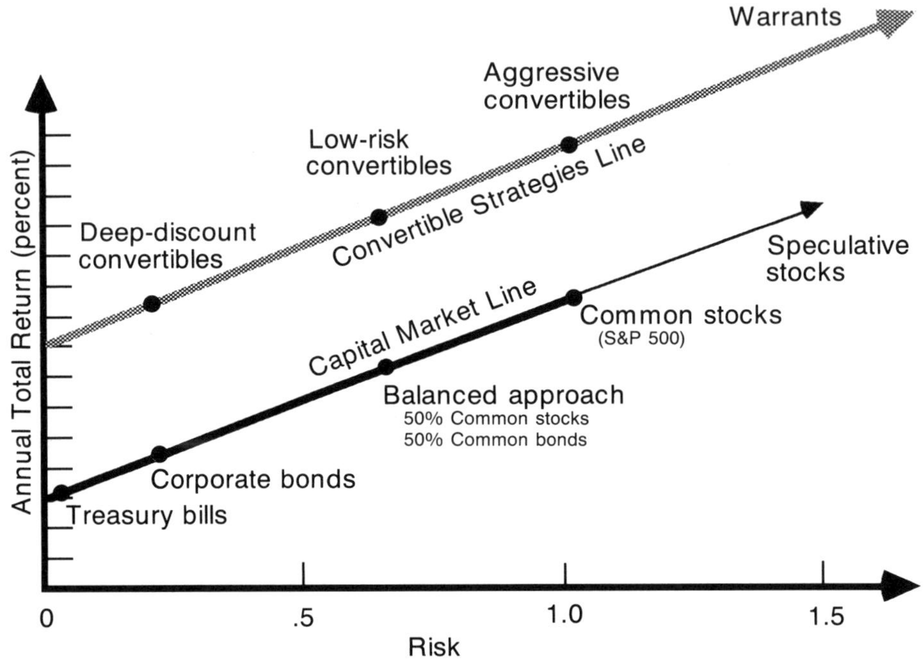

investing with traditional investing. Notice that the convertible strategies line is placed well above the capital market line. This reflects the ability to select issues which are significantly *undervalued.* However, not all convertibles are as attractive as the line suggests. The convertible strategies line shown represents only carefully chosen issues having the most attractive risk-reward features. You will learn how to make these selections in this book.

We will explore the risk-reward characteristics of undervalued convertibles beginning with Chapter 5. First, Chapters 3 and 4 will provide the basics you will need for understanding this highly profitable niche in our nation's financial markets.

CHAPTER 3

The Convertible Alternative

Stocks and bonds are the favorite way U.S. corporations raise new long-term capital. However, companies often use convertible bonds instead of straight bonds or stocks because:

- Convertibles reduce interest costs to the company since they have lower yields than straight bonds.
- Convertibles amount to future sales of stock *above* its current market price.

Numerous factors are weighed by the company and its underwriters when arriving at a new financing decision. Ease of marketing is among these factors. Convertible bonds are in greater demand when the company is doing well.

The number of convertibles on the market has increased over the years as the more glamorous firms chose this low-cost way of borrowing. Recent issues have included such popular areas as energy, high technology, health care, and financial services. Over time, convertibles representing a broad cross section of the overall market have become available. Table 3–1 lists a few of the convertible bonds actively traded on the New York Stock Exchange in mid-1984. Clearly, they are not offered only by low-quality, speculative companies and should not be dismissed on the mistaken assumption that they are.

Table 3–1. Actively traded convertible bonds, June 1984

Company	*Bond Description**
Allied Corp.	7.75 –05
Allied Stores	9.50 –07
American General	11.00 –07
American Medical International	9.50 –01
Barnett Banks of Florida	12.25 –06
Becton Dickinson	10.75 –06
Boeing Co.	8.875–06
Celanese Corp.	9.75 –06
Chase Manhattan Bank	6.50 –96
Deere & Co.	9.00 –08
Denny's	9.50 –07
Eastern Gas & Fuel	9.75 –08
Eastman Kodak	8.25 –07
Federal National Mortgage Association	4.375–96
Ford Motor	4.50 –96
GTE Corp.	10.50 –07
Hercules	6.50 –99
Hospital Corp. America	8.50 –08
Huges Tool Co.	9.50 –06
K mart	6.00 –99
Mapco	10.00 –05
Merrill Lynch & Co.	8.875–07
Mobile	10.50 –08
Northwest Airlines	7.50 –07
Owens-Corning	8.25 –07
Pittson Co.	9.20 –04
RCA Corp.	4.50 –92
Reynolds, R. J.	10.00 –08
Reynolds Metals	4.50 –91
Seagram Co.	8.25 –08
Searle, G. D.	4.50 –92
Signal Companies	5.50 –94

Storer Communications	8.50 –05
Tidewater	7.75 –05
Union Carbide	10.00 –06
U.S. Air Group	9.25 –07
United States Steel	5.75 –01
Walter, Jim	9.00 –07
Western Union	5.25 –97
Xerox	6.00 –95

* Bonds are normally identified by their coupon and an abbreviated maturity date. For example, 7.75–05 means 7.75 percent (at $1,000 par value) maturing in the year 2005. The bond may also be referred to as the 7.75s of 2005; this terminology will be used throughout the text.

CONVERTIBLE BONDS, AN INVESTMENT ALTERNATIVE

Like straight corporate bonds, convertible bonds have fixed interest payments and a maturity date when the issuing company must repay the principal (usually $1,000, although smaller denominations are sometimes issued). However, convertibles provide an additional benefit. The bond may be exchanged for a specified number of common stock shares at the holder's option. As the underlying common stock advances, the convertible bond becomes more valuable. These hybrid securities offer investors an unusual combination of benefits: income, safety, and potential price appreciation.

As an alternative to common stocks, most convertible bonds provide more income and less risk if their stocks decline in price. *These are significant advantages.* Additional advantages are senior status in the company's financial structure, guaranteed income, and par-value redemption at maturity. The risk-reward trade-off is that most convertibles will offer somewhat less capital appreciation than their underlying stocks, upon a price advance. However, some convertibles offer as much upside opportunity as their common stocks, while retaining their inherent low-risk characteristics; *the best of both worlds.* An easy-to-prepare risk-reward analysis will enable you to identify attractive candidates.

Chapter 4 will show you how to evaluate a convertible's risk-reward profile. First, however, you must understand the terminology and the factors that influence prices. *Study the next few pages carefully;* they are easy to follow and will give you the basics essential to understanding how this sector of the financial markets can simultaneously increase return and reduce risk.

INVESTMENT VALUE

A convertible bond's *investment value* is the price at which it would be expected to trade if it did not provide the conversion privilege. Bond-rating services estimate this price just as they evaluate straight bonds. The bond raters consider the convertible's inherent quality and prevailing interest rates for similar securities. Standard & Poor's, for example, assigns a AAA rating to the highest quality bonds and a D rating to those in default. Most convertible bonds fall between these extremes. Those issued by quality companies are usually rated A or BBB; convertibles issued by speculative companies are typically rated B or CCC. Table 3–2 illustrates the relationship between investment value and prevailing interest rates for bonds having a 10 percent coupon and a 20 year life, convertible or nonconvertible.

Table 3–2. Investment value for a 10 percent, 20-year bond versus prevailing long-term interest rates

Interest Rate	*Investment Value*
10%	$1,000
12	850
14	730
16	650
18	570
20	510

Note: Bonds are evaluated and traded in terms of their yield-to-maturity values. Refer to the tables of a *yield book* to determine the precise yield-to-maturity for a given coupon, maturity date, and market price.

To determine a convertible bond's investment value, compare it to a straight bond of similar quality and remaining life. If comparable straight bonds were yielding 16 percent to maturity, a $650 investment value would be assigned to a 10 percent, 20-year convertible bond (see Table 3–2). For a nonconvertible 10 percent bond issued some time ago at par when interest rates were lower, $650 would be its actual market price in order to provide a 16 percent yield-to-maturity. For convertible bonds, the $650 investment value is an important number in evaluating the relationship of risk to reward. However, the convertible's market price is likely to be far higher than $650 because of its convertibility.

Consider a hypothetical convertible bond, High-Tech Industries, with a 10 percent coupon and 20 year life, maturing in the year 2004. The bond terms and price relationships that follow are representative of typical new convertibles issued by aggressive growth companies in mid-1984. I chose an aggressive convertible bond for my example (instead of a high-quality selection like those in Table 3–1) because it will be more appropriate for illustrating different strategies throughout the book. However, the discussion that follows applies to all convertible bonds.

The $650 investment value (the horizontal line of Exhibit 3–1) is the

Exhibit 3–1. Investment value: High-Tech Industries 10 percent, 20-year convertible bond (yield-to-maturity = 16 percent)

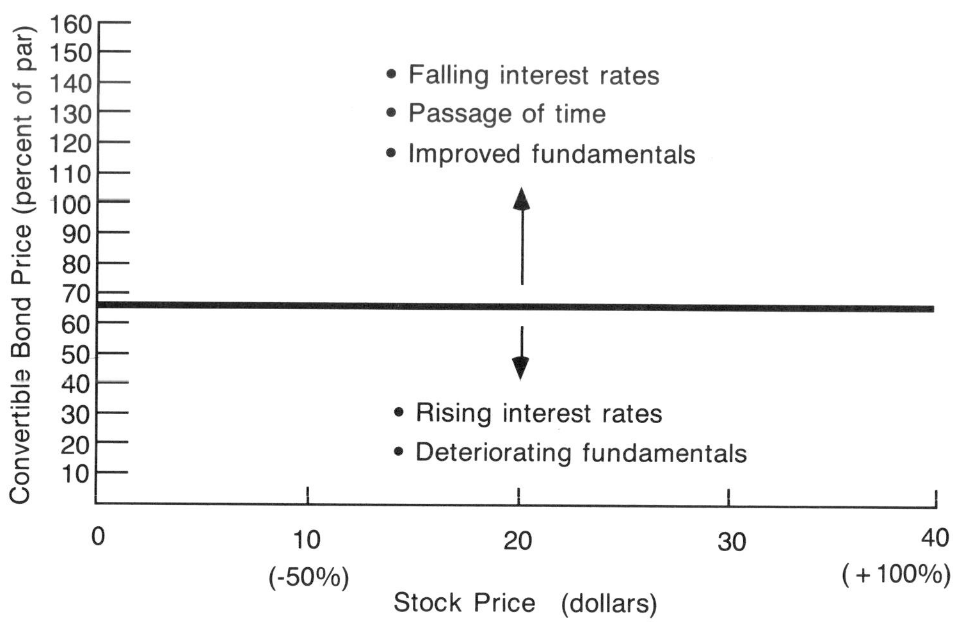

first step toward preparing a risk-reward analysis for High-Tech's 10s of 2004. Notice that bond prices, shown on the vertical axis of the exhibit, are expressed as a percent of par. Thus 65 (dollar sign intentionally omitted) means 65 percent of $1,000, or $650. From this point on, I will frequently use this traditional shorthand when quoting bond prices.

In theory, the investment value of 65 is independent of the stock's price, shown on the horizontal axis of Exhibit 3–1. This is why the graph is flat. However, if the stock declined sharply, it might indicate deteriorating fundamentals within the company. In that event, the investment values for all High-Tech Industries' senior securities, including its convertibles, might have to be downgraded. While the rating services are often slow to reevaluate a troubled company, the market usually reacts quickly to changing conditions.

Of more immediate concern for most convertible bonds is the impact of fluctuating interest rates on investment values. If prevailing long-term rates were to advance from 16 percent to 20 percent, for example, the investment value for High-Tech's 10s of 2004 would drop by nearly a fourth from 65 to 51 (Table 3–2). Conversely, declining interest rates would cause the investment value to rise, as would the passage of time; it must advance to full par value (100) on the bond's maturity date. Other factors, such as acquisition of High-Tech by a financially stronger company, could also cause the investment value to rise.

A convertible bond's investment value is often referred to as a price "floor," the price below which the bond cannot fall regardless of how much its common stock declines. If a convertible bond's price dropped below its investment value floor, conventional fixed-income investors would be quick to purchase it; they would receive the valuable convertibility feature at no cost. This concept of a price floor is an important tool when preparing a risk-reward analysis, as I will show in Chapter 4. However, always keep in mind the factors that could cause significant fluctuations in the future: interest rate changes, fundamental changes, and the passage of time.

CONVERSION VALUE

When issued, every convertible bond is assigned a *conversion ratio,* the number of common stock shares for which it can be exchanged. The exchange privilege is at the bondholder's option and normally extends throughout the bond's life. The bond's *conversion value* is its conversion ratio multiplied by the common stock's current market price. This calculation represents the convertible's worth if it is exchanged for common stock and the shares are immediately sold.

Assuming a conversion ratio of 40 shares for the High-Tech 10s of 2004, the conversion value is shown as the sloping straight line of Exhibit 3–2. For example, if the stock is trading at $20 per share, the conversion value is 80 ($800):

$$40 \text{ shares} \times \$20 \text{ per share} = \$800$$

If the stock doubled to $40, the conversion value would also increase 100 percent to 160 ($1,600); if it declined by 50 percent, the conversion value would also halve.

Since conversion value is the bond's worth if the holder exchanged

Exhibit 3–2. Conversion value: High-Tech Industries 10 percent, 20-year convertible bond (conversion ratio = 40 shares)

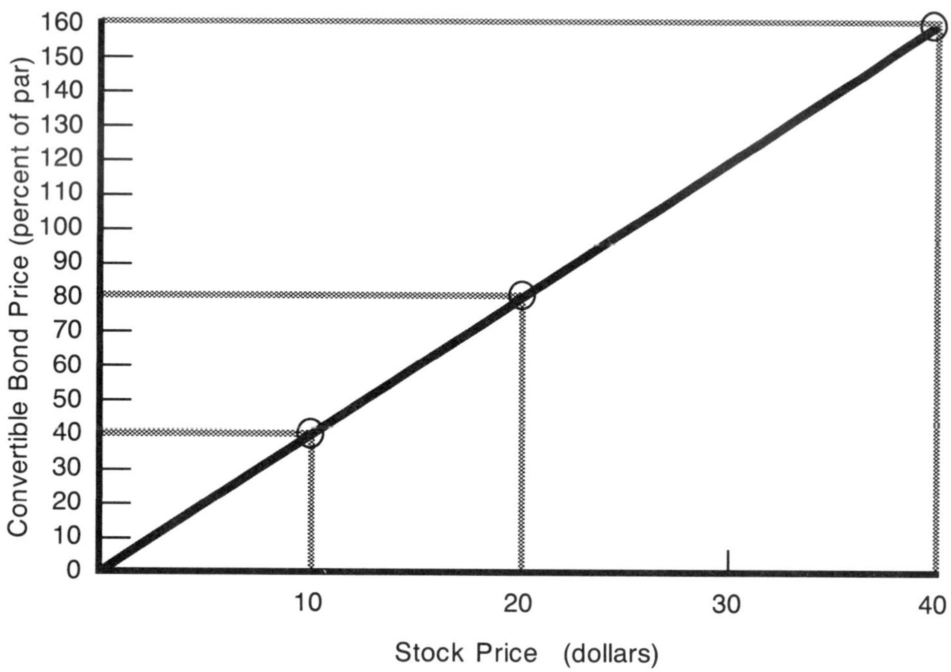

it for common stock, any convertible should trade at or above its conversion value. Otherwise, professional arbitragers would profit by purchasing the bond while simultaneously selling the underlying common stock. As an example, if the High-Tech bond was trading at only 155 when its common stock was at $40, arbitragers would buy the bond for $1,550 and sell 40 shares of stock for $1,600. They would earn a $50 risk-free profit for every bond purchased.

Convertibles are often described as having a *conversion price,* the price at which the common stock must sell for the bond to be worth par value if converted. The more useful tool, conversion ratio, is determined by dividing the conversion price into $1,000 (par value). For High-Tech Industries, the conversion price is $25 and the conversion ratio is 40 shares ($1,000 ÷ $25 per share = 40 shares).

Exhibit 3–3 combines the investment value line of Exhibit 3–1 and the conversion value line of Exhibit 3–2. Since a convertible should always

Exhibit 3–3. Price boundaries: High-Tech Industries 10 percent, 20-year convertible bond

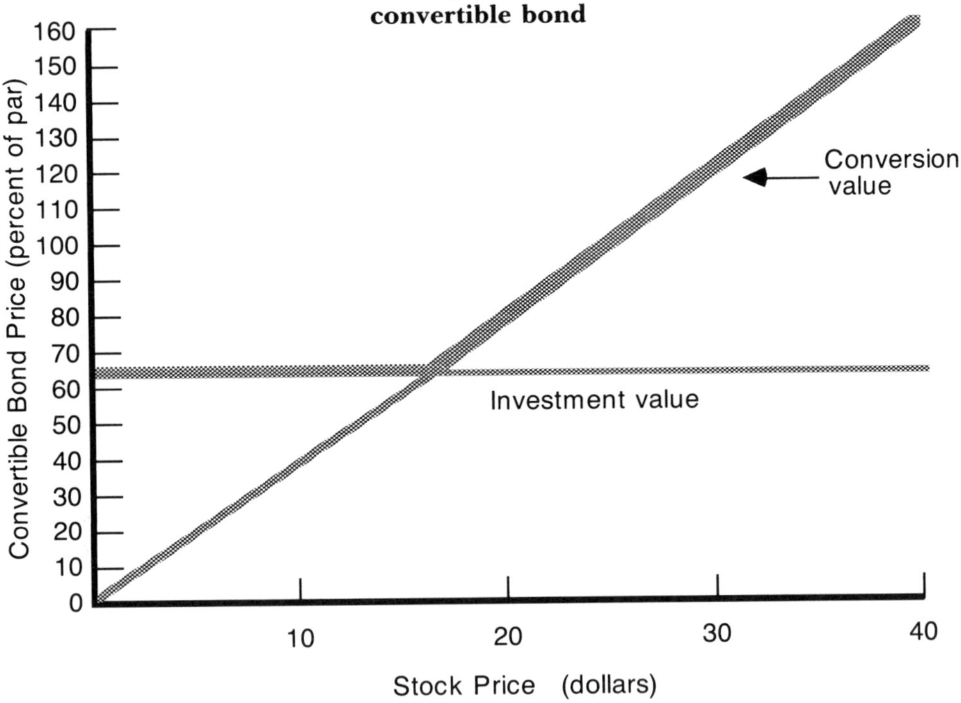

sell at a price above both its investment value and its conversion value, the heavy portions of the two lines represent minimum bond prices for all future stock prices.

THE CONVERTIBLE PRICE CURVE

Exhibit 3–4 repeats the investment value and conversion value lines of Exhibit 3–3 and introduces the concept of a *convertible price curve,* a curve showing the expected price for High-Tech's convertible at any stock price in the near future. This very important curve will permit us to determine whether the convertible bond is an attractive alternative to

Exhibit 3–4. The convertible price curve: High-Tech Industries 10 percent, 20-year bond (conversion ratio = 40 shares, straight bond equivalent yield = 16 percent)

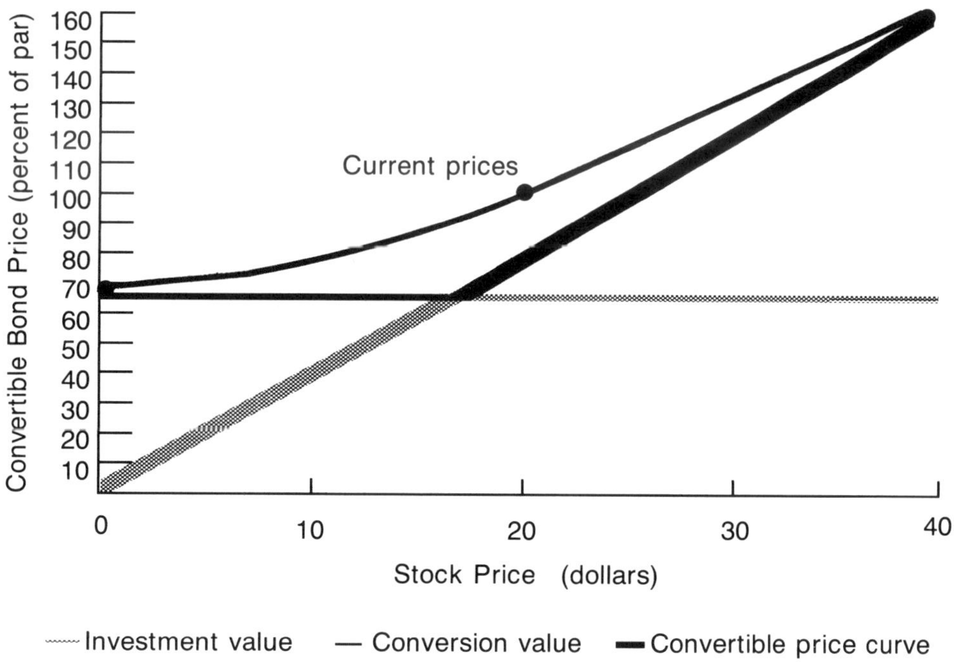

traditional stocks and bonds. *It is the most important concept you will learn in this book.*

There are complex formulas available for modeling the curve, but here is a convenient approximation that is sufficiently accurate for our purposes. As shown by Exhibit 3–4, the price curve passes through current market prices for the two securities, shown as 100 for the bond and $20 for the common stock. The lowest point on the curve appears when it strikes the investment value line, the bond's price floor of 65, at a price of $0 for the common stock. A third point, necessary for modeling the curve, is more subjective. Here one's experience must be brought into play, recognizing that as convertible bonds advance to well above par, most companies will call them in at a price slightly above par. Since a call forces the bondholder to exchange his fixed-income security for common stock to assure receiving full conversion value, the bond will lose any premium and trade on its conversion value line. For the High-Tech issue, I assumed it would trade at conversion value when it reached 160 (with the common stock at $40). The convertible price curve of Exhibit 3–4 was drawn by connecting the three points with a curved ruler.

We can now prepare a risk-reward analysis. However, you will be better equipped if you first study some additional tools commonly used by convertible specialists.

POPULAR TOOLS FOR EVALUATING CONVERTIBLES

In addition to investment value, conversion ratio, and conversion value, you will need four other concepts which are important when evaluating convertibles and communicating with others in the convertible securities market. They are not complex. Take a few minutes to become comfortable with them.

Conversion premium. A convertible's premium over its conversion value (conversion premium) is an important tool for measuring worth. At a price of 100, with the underlying stock trading at $20, the High-Tech bond's conversion premium is 25 percent.

$$\text{Conversion value} = 40 \text{ shares} \times \$20 \text{ per share} = \$800$$

$$\text{Conversion premium} = \frac{\$1{,}000 - \$800}{\$800} = \frac{\$200}{\$800} = 25\%$$

When the conversion premium is low, the convertible will respond more readily to a price advance by its common stock. Thus, bonds with low conversion premiums offer greater opportunity.

Investment value premium. A convertible's premium over its investment value (investment value premium) is also an important tool in the risk-reward analysis. At a price of 100, the High-Tech bond's investment value premium is 54 percent.

$$\text{Investment value} = \$650$$

$$\text{Investment value premium} = \frac{\$1{,}000 - \$650}{\$650} = \frac{\$350}{\$650} = 54\%$$

When the investment value premium is low, the convertible is less likely to drop sharply upon a price decline by its common stock. Thus, bonds with low investment value premiums offer less risk.

Yield advantage. Assuming High-Tech's common stock pays no dividend, the yield advantage for the convertible is 10 percent.

$$\begin{aligned} \text{Convertible bond's current yield} &= \frac{\$100}{\$1{,}000} = 10.0\% \\ \text{Minus stock yield} &= \underline{\quad 0 \quad} \\ \text{Yield advantage} &= 10.0\% \end{aligned}$$

Most new convertibles provide higher yields than their underlying common stocks. As time passes, the yield advantage will diminish if the stock's dividend is increased, since the convertible's cash payout remains fixed throughout its life.

Break-even time. Another analytical tool is the number of years it will take for the convertible's yield advantage to recover the conversion premium. Assuming equal $1,000 investments in the convertible bond and the non-dividend-paying common stock, the break-even time is calculated as follows:

Market value of bond	$1,000
Conversion value (40 shares × $20)	− 800
Conversion premium	$ 200
Yearly income from bond	$ 100
Yearly income from 50 shares of stock	− 0
Income advantage	$ 100

$$\text{Break-even time} = \frac{\text{Conversion premium}}{\text{Income advantage}} = \frac{\$200}{\$100} = 2.0 \text{ years}$$

Break-even time is probably the most popular tool of professional convertible bond buyers. They consider recovery of the conversion premium in less than three years to be favorable. However, none of these tools can stand alone. Chapter 4 will show you how to identify attractive issues.

TYPICAL NEW CONVERTIBLE BOND ISSUES

Convertible bonds are used by many different companies to raise capital. Even IBM had a convertible bond issue registered with the Securities and Exchange Commission in mid-1982. But when long-term interest rates began to decline sharply, they withdrew the registration in favor of straight debt. The proposed IBM convertible would have been the largest issue ever ($500 million) and would have enhanced the prestige of the convertible bond market. Table 3–3 presents data showing typical convertible bonds which came to the market during 1983.

The *low-risk* category represents good quality firms such as most of those listed in Table 3–1. The *aggressive* category represents more speculative companies. Note the difference in issue size between the two types ($100 million versus $20 million). Low-risk convertibles have much greater market liquidity and are typically traded on the New York Stock Exchange. Aggressive convertibles are usually traded on the American Stock Exchange or the Over-the-Counter Market.

Notice also the differences in yield advantage (4 percent versus 10 percent) and conversion premium (15 percent versus 25 percent) between the two groups. Most issues have a mixture of these indicated characteris-

Table 3–3. Typical new convertible bond issues, 1983

	Low-Risk	*Aggressive*
Price	100	100
Interest rate	8%	10%
Years-to-maturity	20	20
Issue size, $ million	100	20
Yield advantage	4%	10%
Conversion premium	15%	25%
S&P investment grade	A	B
Straight bond equivalent yield	12%	16%
Investment value	70	65
Investment value premium	43%	54%

tics. As I stated earlier, convertible bonds cover the entire market spectrum, allowing investors with widely different risk tolerances to construct convertible portfolios that meet their specific risk-reward objectives.

BONDS WITH WARRANTS ATTACHED

Another way companies raise capital is by issuing straight bonds with *warrants* attached. Shortly after these instruments come to the market, the two securities are separated and trade independently of each other.

A warrant is generally defined as a security which gives the holder the right to purchase common stock directly from the company on specified terms and within a given period, typically 3–5 years. Their straight bonds can usually be tendered at their par value, in lieu of cash, when exercising the warrants. Warrants, by themselves, are highly speculative instruments. They can produce large capital gains or expire worthless. When combined with their usable straight bonds, the *unit* acquires low-risk investment characteristics much as those of a convertible bond.

Warrants were popular during the go-go days of the 60s when conglomerates employed them as *sweeteners* to other securities issued when acquiring companies. They were referred to as "funny money" when conglomerates later fell out of favor in the 70s. Recently, however, warrants have been enjoying a strong comeback as corporate treasurers search for ways to lower the cost of new capital. A 36 million share issue was marketed in 1983 by MCI Communications via a $1 billion package of bonds and warrants. This bond/warrant issue was larger than any convertible bond offering to date.

Despite their speculative nature, warrants may be combined with other instruments for controlling portfolio risk. Low-risk/high-return warrant strategies will be presented in Chapter 10.

CONVERTIBLE PREFERREDS

Unlike convertible bonds issued by companies to raise new funds, *convertible preferreds* usually come to the market via acquisitions. The shareholders of the company being acquired do not have an immediate tax liability if they receive new common or preferred stock (equity securities) in exchange for their original common shares. If they receive cash or debt instruments, their original shares would be treated as having been sold at the time of the exchange for tax purposes. Since the target company is frequently in a position to strike a hard bargain, it negotiates a higher-yielding and higher-quality convertible preferred in lieu of common. The disadvantage to the company issuing the preferred is that dividends are paid from after-tax profits, whereas bond interest is fully tax-deductible to the corporation.

Since convertible bonds and convertible preferreds have many similar characteristics, both may be evaluated on such factors as conversion premium, investment value premium, and yield advantage. As I use the term "convertible" in later chapters, you may apply it to both bonds and preferreds. However, keep in mind that bonds are safer and approaching maturity dates can provide important price support as their investment floors rise toward par.

Table 3–4 presents a representative list of actively traded convertible preferreds listed on the New York Stock Exchange in mid-1984.

SPECIAL SITUATIONS

So far, I have described convertibles that represent the largest segment of the convertible securities market. However, there are other issues

Table 3–4. Actively traded convertible preferreds, June 1984

Company	*Preferred Description**
American General	$2.64 D
Anheuser-Bush	3.60 A
Armco	2.10
Ashland Oil	3.96
Avco	3.20
Beatrice Foods	3.38 A
Bethlehem Steel	2.50
Boise Cascade	5.00 B
CIGNA	2.75 A
Champion International	4.60
Chemical New York	1.875
City Investing	2.875 E
Cooper Industries	2.90
Crown Zellerbach	4.625 A
Diamond Shamrock	4.00
Esmark	2.80 B
Fairchild Industries	3.60
Household International	6.25
ITT Corp.	5.00 O
Jewel Cos.	2.31 A
Kaiser Cement	1.375
Lear Petroleum	2.875
Libbey-Owens-Ford	4.75
Martin Marietta	4.875
McDermott International	2.20
Northwest Natural Gas	2.375
Ohio Edison	1.80
Penn Central	5.27
Reading & Bates	2.125
RepublicBank Corp.	2.125 A
Sybron	2.40
Textron	2.08 A

Table 3–4. (*Cont.*)

Company	*Preferred Description**
Trans World Corp.	2.66 C
UAL Inc.	2.40 B
Union Pacific	7.25 A
United Technologies	2.55
U.S. Life	2.25 D
Washington National	2.50
Weyerhaeuser	2.80
Woolworth, F. W.	2.20 A

* Preferred stocks are normally identified by their annual dividend payments. If two different issues carry the same dividend, letters are added to distinguish the differences (e.g., $2.00 pfd A and $2.00 pfd B).

that offer either greater opportunities for the alert investor or hidden traps for the unwary. All convertible investors should be able to evaluate these unusual situations. To help you do so, I have included Appendix A at the end of this book.

The following chapters will provide important instructions for evaluating candidates and for building and managing a portfolio of selected low-risk securities. Before proceeding, however, I urge you to master the basic concepts and terms presented so far. They will help you understand the low-risk/high-performance investment strategies soon to be presented.

CHAPTER 4

The Profit Profile

New convertible bond offerings are purchased predominantly by institutional money managers: banks, insurance companies, and investment advisors. Since most of these money-management professionals view convertibles as a low-risk alternative to owning common stocks, they place them in equity portfolios, instead of portfolios of fixed-income securities. Other more sophisticated managers look at them as the hybrid securities they are, and construct separate convertible securities portfolios.

Working through institutional stockbrokers at major brokerage firms at the time of the offering, underwriters representing the company negotiate the issue's terms with prospective buyers. Buyers are looking for the highest coupon and lowest conversion premium they can obtain; a low conversion premium means more shares when the convertibles are exchanged for common stock later. The company, on the other hand, desires financing at the lowest possible interest cost with the highest conversion premium possible (fewer shares reduce future stock dilution). A deal is struck and the final terms are announced. How do the buyers of new convertible bond issues make their decisions?

Let's go back to the hypothetical convertible bond presented in Chapter 3. The High-Tech Industries 10s of 2004 bond is typical of the new issues often marketed by small growth companies in need of capital. Some strategies are best for aggressive convertibles, such as the High-Tech, and some are best for high-quality issues. This chapter's discussion applies to all convertibles, aggressive and high-quality alike.

NEW-ISSUE RISK-REWARD ANALYSIS

Most professionals purchasing traditional securities such as stocks and bonds employ either fundamental or technical analysis (or both) when making their investment decisions. After studying a company thoroughly, they may conclude that its common stock or straight bonds have more upside opportunity than downside risk. They may then decide to buy. Convertible specialists go a step further. In addition to a favorable determination on the company under consideration, they evaluate the convertible independently. Their objective is to determine whether the convertible offers any advantages over purchasing the common stock, or a combination of stock and bonds as in the balanced approach. Here is how they would arrive at their investment decision for the new High-Tech convertible bond.

Exhibit 4–1. The convertible price curve: High-Tech Industries 10 percent, 20-year bond (conversion ratio = 40 shares, straight bond equivalent yield = 16 percent)

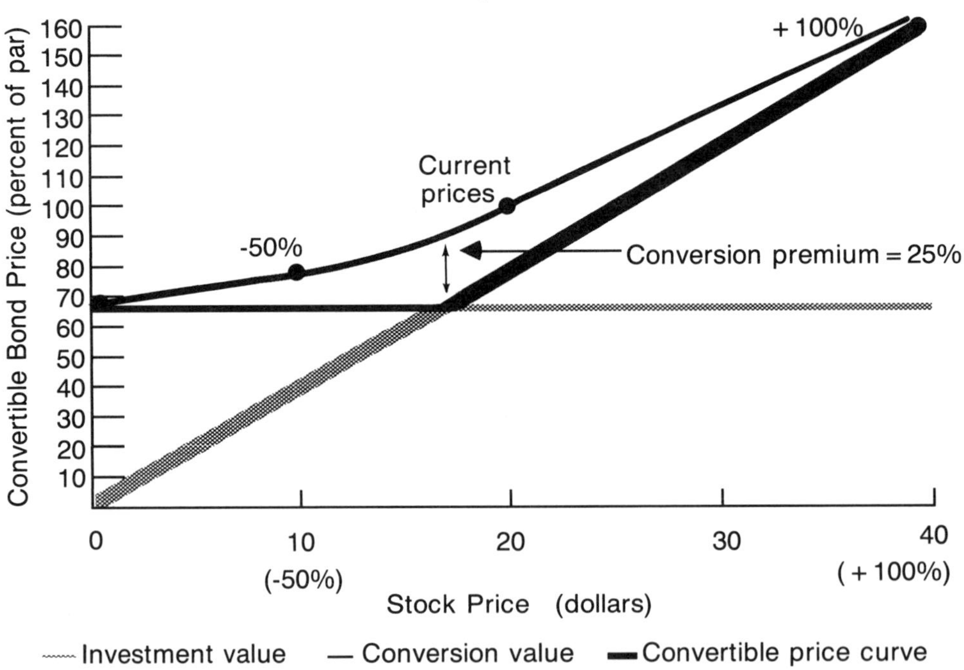

Exhibit 4–1 repeats the price curve for High-Tech's convertible and highlights expected bond prices for stock price moves of −50 percent and +100 percent (roughly equal probabilities). This broad price range should encompass future prices for most common stocks over a one-year period, the usual time frame for our risk-reward analyses. On the downside, if the common stock dropped 50 percent, from $20 to $10, the convertible bond would be expected to decline 22 percent, from par to 78. For a 100 percent stock price advance to $40, the bond would be expected to post a 60 percent gain by trading at 160. These price relationships are typical of all new convertible issues. There is less risk, but there is also less upside opportunity. However, by themselves, the numbers are inconclusive. Is the downside risk-reduction an adequate trade-off for reduced appreciation potential? How should the convertible's 10 percent yield advantage be evaluated?

CONVERTIBLE BONDS VERSUS COMMON STOCK

The risk-reward analysis of Table 4–1 begins to bring the price relationships into perspective. Assuming a one-year holding period, *total returns* (income plus capital gains or losses) for High-Tech's common stock and convertible bonds are compared over a broad span of possible future

Table 4–1. Risk-reward analysis: High-Tech Industries 10s of 2004 at 100 versus common stock at $20

	Stock Price Change in 12 Months		
	−50 Percent	*0 Percent*	*+100 Percent*
Common stock			
Capital gain or loss	−50%	0%	+100%
Dividends received	0	0	0
Total Return	−50%	0%	+100%
Convertible bond			
Capital gain or loss	−22%	0%	+ 60%
Interest received	+10	+10	+ 10
Total return	−12%	+10%	+ 70%
Convertible advantage	+38%	+10%	− 30%

stock prices ranging from $10 to $40 per share. Since the risk-reward calculations include the convertible's 10 percent yield advantage for one year, this income adds to its upside potential and reduces its downside risk.

As you can see, the convertible bond's total return provides more than two thirds of the common's upside opportunity (70 versus 100 percent) at about one fourth the downside risk (−12 versus −50 percent). In addition, bondholders would enjoy a steady 10 percent income stream in a sideways (static) market, when the stockholders would receive nothing. It would seem that the convertible bond might be the superior choice, but perhaps a combination of stock and higher-yielding straight bonds at 16 percent would be better than the convertible. Remember, a convertible should be purchased only if it offers risk-reward opportunities that are superior to a combination of conventional stocks and bonds.

CONVERTIBLE BONDS VERSUS THE BALANCED APPROACH

Table 4–2 compares the convertible bond with the balanced approach, 50 percent common stock and 50 percent straight bonds at 16 percent yield. The analysis assumes that long-term interest rates remain constant over the next year. Thus, neither the convertible nor the straight bond

Table 4–2. Risk-reward analysis: High-Tech Industries 10s of 2004 at 100 versus common stock at $20 and straight bonds at 16 percent

	Stock Price Change in 12 Months		
	−50 Percent	*0 Percent*	*+100 Percent*
Balanced approach			
Common stock	−50%	0%	+100%
Straight bonds	+16	+16	+ 16
50% stock/50% bonds	−17%	+ 8%	+ 58%
Convertible bond			
Capital gain or loss	−22%	0%	+ 60%
Interest received	+10	+10	+ 10
Total return	−12%	+10%	+ 70%
Convertible advantage	+ 5%	+ 2%	+ 12%

will be affected by a changing interest rate climate for this analysis. (The impact of interest rate changes is evaluated in Appendix B.)

The risk-reward analysis conclusively demonstrates the convertible bond's advantages over conventional securities. The convertible would be expected to provide higher returns (or less risk) at any future stock price than the balanced approach of stocks and straight bonds. The one year advantage ranges from 2 percent in a static market to 5 percent on the downside and 12 percent on the upside. These are very significant benefits. We are well on our way toward a low-risk/high-performance investment program.

PROFIT PROFILES

Exhibits 4–2 and 4–3 graph the results of our risk-reward calculations for the High-Tech securities (Tables 4–1 and 4–2) as *profit profiles.* Profit

Exhibit 4–2. Profit profiles: High-Tech Industries 10s of 2004 versus common stock

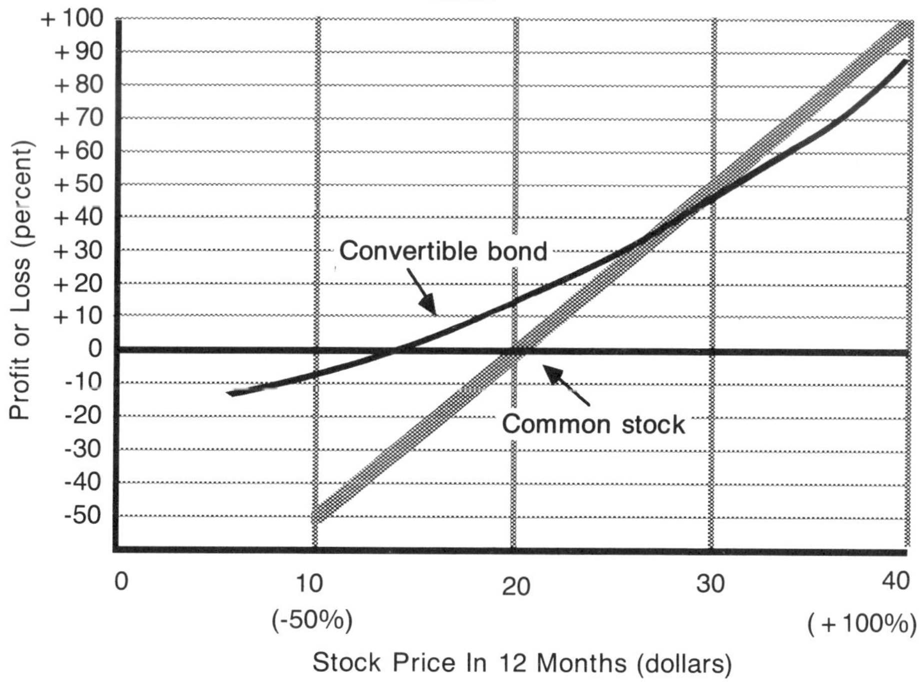

profiles permit a visual comparison of investment alternatives. They illustrate the relative merits of different strategies better than a risk-reward analysis table since gains or losses can be quickly ascertained for any future stock price. Exhibit 4–2, shows the common stock providing greater profit for a 12-month price advance above $24, while the convertible bond offers a higher return (or less risk) at any stock price below $24. Profit profiles are useful portfolio-management tools for comparing alternative investments at all possible outcomes.

Upon looking at the profit profiles of Exhibit 4–2, many investors would reject the High-Tech convertible because it is destined to underperform its common at all prices above $24. Having been sold a good story, they may be "certain" the stock will quickly rise to $40 a share, or higher. They have likely forgotten, or never learned that controlling risk is an important aspect of successful investing. Even though "happiness may be a stock that doubles," stocks are just as likely to go down. Suppose that an investor owned three stocks such as High-Tech in his portfolio and one doubled while the other two both dropped in half over the next year. The two 50 percent losers would offset the single 100 percent winner for a net break-even. On the other hand, an investor who owned three convertibles such as High-Tech's would wind up with a net profit of 15 percent (the average of +70 percent, −12 percent and −12 percent). *Which investor would you rather be?*

The profit profiles of Exhibit 4–3 compare the High-Tech convertible with the 50/50 balanced approach of stocks and bonds. Here, we can see the convertible's advantages beyond any doubt. It outperforms the balanced approach at all future stock prices, with the advantage widening for extreme stock price movements.

UNDERVALUED SECURITIES

By my definition, when a convertible security exhibits risk-reward advantages over conventional securities (stocks, bonds, or money market instruments in any combination appropriate for analysis), I call the convertible *undervalued.* It is undervalued in terms of logic and simple mathematics, not because of someone's opinion of the company or forecast of the future. Both fundamental and technical analysis may have important roles to play in the investment decision, but that analysis applies to the company

Exhibit 4–3. Profit profiles: High-Tech Industries 10s of 2004 versus the balanced approach

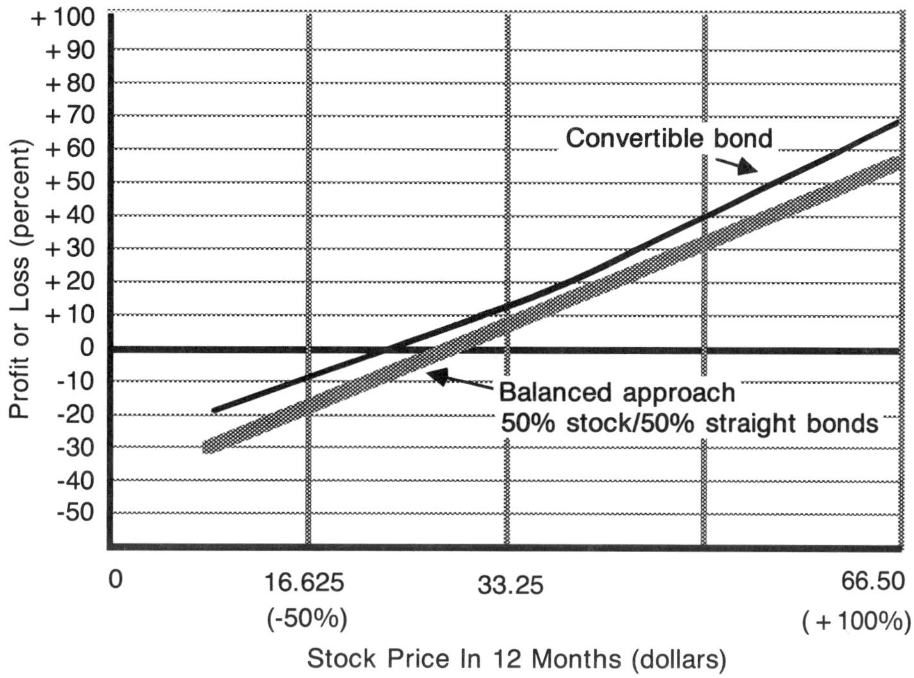

itself. The convertible analysis comes afterward for the purpose of identifying it as a *superior alternative.*

A direct comparison of the High-Tech convertible with its common stock was inconclusive; there were times when the stock would outperform the convertible. The significant comparison was against a combination of stock and bonds, recognizing that a convertible bond is a hybrid of both. (The convertible outperformed the combination at all possible outcomes.) This may inconvenience investors who think only in terms of equity or fixed income and are unable or unwilling to evaluate hybrids or money managers and consultants who are not willing or unable to sell the concept of hybrid securities to their institutional clients.

For instance, I have often heard market professionals state that convertibles are the *worst* of both worlds. They advise avoidance of convertibles because:

1. As an alternative to common stock, they offer less upside opportunity, and
2. As an alternative to straight bonds, they provide less income.

Both observations are correct, as shown by our risk-reward analyses and profit profiles. But what should be obvious to the aware investor is: *investment success requires thoughtful evaluation of risk-reward trade-offs.* To state that convertibles are bad because they won't advance as much as their common stock, disregards their higher yield and greater safety. To state that convertibles are bad because they yield less than straight bonds, disregards their ability to provide capital appreciation when their stocks rise in value. A risk-reward analysis as that of Table 4–1 or 4–2 is an essential prelude to any intelligent decision.

Professionals who avoid convertibles, a suprising number of whom are large institutional money managers and consultants, continue to build balanced portfolios of common stocks and straight bonds. Their conventional portfolios provide less income *and* less capital appreciation than would a typical convertible securities portfolio.

I firmly believe the "truths" we frequently accept without question are often wrong. As you read this book, I urge you to go back to the basics and reexamine your own beliefs about investing. Thoughtful skepticism is a trait which, I suspect, is shared by all successful investors.

WHY ARE NEW CONVERTIBLE ISSUES UNDERVALUED?

Since the High-Tech 10s of 2004 provided risk-reward advantages as most new convertible bonds, we can reasonably conclude that the new-issue convertible bond market is undervalued. This conclusion flies in the face of efficient market proponents who believe all securities are properly priced relative to each other. They advise that no advantages can be gained through careful research. Therefore, why not just throw darts at the financial pages?

While it is not my intention to refute the theory of efficient markets as it pertains to conventional stocks and bonds, the theory is *dead wrong* when it confronts the markets for convertible securities. You have seen some evidence of this with our High-Tech example; you will see considerably more evidence as I present low-risk/high-reward strategies in the following chapters.

The undervaluation of new-issue convertibles is not mysterious. All new issues are predominantly purchased by highly sophisticated professionals who know what they are doing. They know also that when trading commences in the aftermarkets, selling their million dollar positions, if this is what they want to do, will not be easy. The aftermarket for most convertibles is not as liquid as it is for stocks and bonds. Poor trading liquidity is a major handicap for the large money managers who typically handle funds in excess of a billion dollars. For this reason, they insist on receiving compensating risk-reward advantages when buying the newly-issued convertibles, and their demands are usually met. Smaller investors can gain the same risk-reward advantages without being burdened by the problem of trading huge position sizes. The convertible securities market is an ideal investment arena for investors of less than institutional size. Smaller investors can also gain even greater benefits through careful selection of aftermarket bargains. Let's proceed to Chapter 5 to find out how.

CHAPTER 5

Undervalued Opportunities for Individual Investors

New convertible bond issues *are* usually undervalued. That is, they are good buys, for they enjoy risk-reward advantages over both common stocks and straight bonds. These advantages are provided because institutional buyers demand added sweeteners to offset the poor trading liquidity they expect in the aftermarket. The sweeteners may take the form of higher interest rates and higher conversion ratios.

Even with such added sweeteners, institutional investors can have trouble unloading large amounts of convertible bonds if they need cash or if the bonds' attractiveness declines. To illustrate, consider the dilemma a bank trust officer might face after purchasing a million dollars' worth of the High-Tech 10s of 2004. The investment decision had been supported by his research department's favorable analysis of the company. Suddenly, however, Research changes its outlook for the company's future and urges the sale of all High-Tech securities held by the bank: common stock, straight bonds, and convertible bonds alike. Common stock and straight bonds can usually be sold without disrupting the markets to any great extent. For the convertible bonds, the question becomes: sell to whom?

AFTERMARKET BARGAINS

Upon receipt of the sale directive, the trust officer asks his trading desk to contact the bank's stockbrokers (major brokerage firms having active institutional trading departments). The brokers attempt a swap with another institutional client at a price reasonably close to the last traded price on the exchange where the convertible is listed. If successful, the order is crossed away from the exchange. (Price and volume are never reported for off-board bond trades, where most bond trading activity takes place.) However, suppose that other portfolio managers have reached similar negative opinions on the outlook for High-Tech Industries. Perhaps they may be attempting to sell their large positions as well; there may be no ready buyers. What happens next?

As with any product subject to the economic laws of supply and demand, the bond's price must be reduced to encourage buyers. After all, there are usually investors who will disagree with anyone's opinions in the securities markets and who would be willing to acquire the convertibles, especially if they become available at bargain prices. As the bond's price is lowered, more and more buyers are attracted. For analytical purposes, let's assume the price is ultimately reduced to 90 with its common stock at $20, as it was when the bond was originally issued at par. This sale at 90 could take place shortly after issuance or years later. For direct comparison with the risk-reward analyses of Chapter 4, we will assume the bond still has 20 years of remaining life.

The graph of Exhibit 5–1 is similar to the High-Tech convertible price curve of Exhibit 4–1. The difference is that the bond's current price is now 90, not 100. As shown, the 10 point price reduction cuts the conversion premium in half, to 12.5 percent versus the original 25 percent. The High-Tech bond is obviously a better purchase at 90 than at 100. But, how much better?

The new convertible price curve (Exhibit 5–1) is again constructed by smoothly connecting three points: current prices, a bond price of 65 at $0 for the stock, and a bond price of 160 at a stock price of $40. The new curve shows the same 160 price objective for a 100 percent stock advance, but the convertible's gain increases from 60 percent up to 78 percent since it starts at 90 instead of 100. On the downside, the new curve shows the bond dropping to 72 (at a stock price of $10),

Exhibit 5–1 The convertible price curve: High-Tech Industries 10s of 2004 trading at 90 (conversion ratio = 40 shares, straight bond equivalent yield = 16 percent)

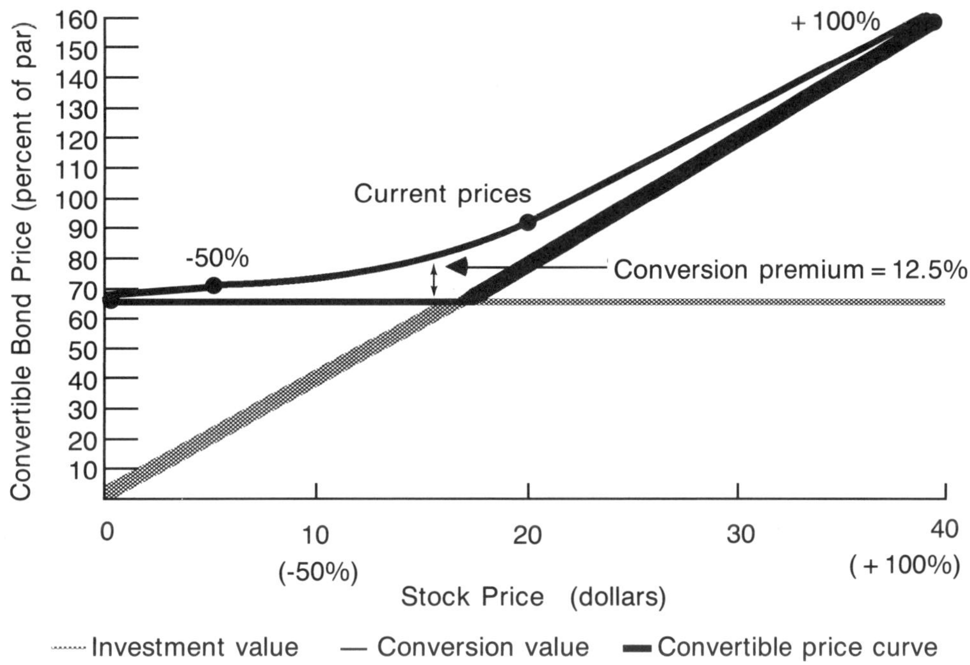

compared to 78 for the original analysis. This conservative approach assumes the bond will remain quite undervalued over the near term, although prices could bounce back to a higher curve once the selling pressure subsides. Moreover, the 20 percent potential decline from 90 down to 72 is less than our original 22 percent estimate, from 100 down to 78. In addition to greater upside opportunity at less downside risk, the convertible's 10 percent coupon provides a higher 11.1 percent current yield at the lower bond price of 90.

Tables 5–1 and 5–2 and Exhibit 5–2 present risk-reward calculations and profit profiles similar to those studied in Chapter 4 when the bond was issued at par. Notice the improvements: For example, the convertible offers nearly as much upside opportunity as its higher-risk common stock, 89 percent versus 100 percent over a one-year period.

Table 5–1. Risk-reward analysis: High-Tech Industries 10s of 2004 at 90 versus common stock at $20

	Stock Price Change in 12 Months		
	−50 Percent	*0 Percent*	*+100 Percent*
Common stock			
Capital gain or loss	−50%	0%	+100%
Dividends received	0	0	0
Total return	−50%	0%	+100%
Convertible bond			
Capital gain or loss	−20%	0%	+ 78%
Interest received	+11	+11	+11
Total return	− 9%	+11%	+ 89%
Convertible advantage	+41%	+11%	− 11%

Table 5–2. Risk-reward analysis: High-Tech Industries 10s of 2004 at 90 versus the balanced approach (common stock at $20 and straight bonds at 16%)

	Stock Price Change in 12 Months		
	−50 Percent	*0 Percent*	*+100 Percent*
Balanced approach			
Common stock	−50%	0%	+100%
Straight bonds	+16	+16	+ 16
50% stock/50% bonds	−17%	+ 8%	+ 58%
Convertible bond			
Capital gain or loss	−20%	0%	+ 78%
Interest received	+11	+11	+ 11
Total return	− 9%	+11%	+ 89%
Convertible advantage	+ 8%	+ 3%	+ 31%

Exhibit 5–2. Profit profiles: High-Tech Industries 10s of 2004 purchased at 90 versus common stock and the balanced approach

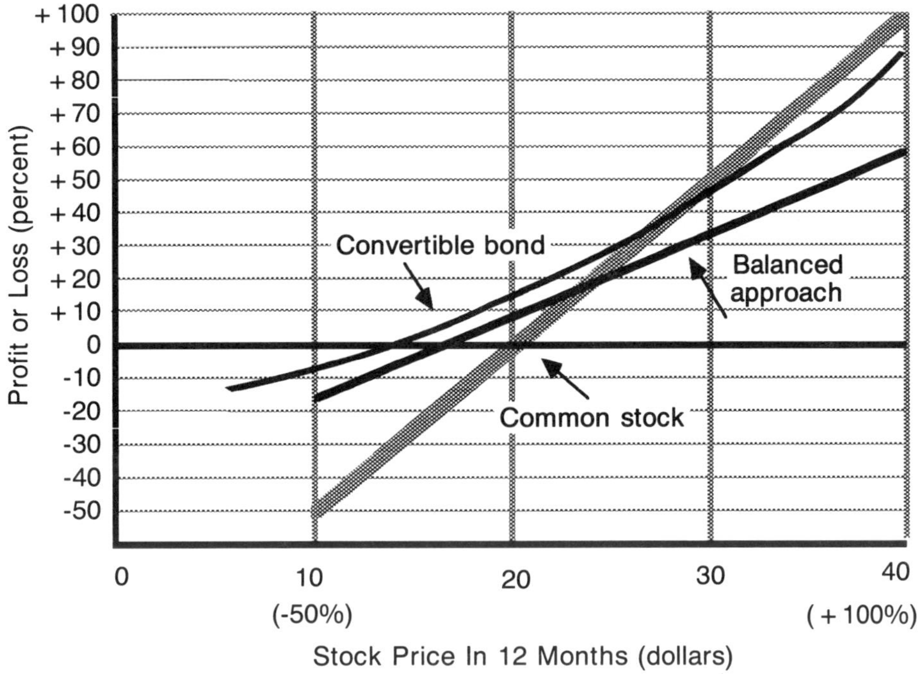

Since there is nothing magical about our one year assumption and since most stocks do not double in a year, how would the comparison look for longer holding periods? If we add the bond's 11.1 percent current yield for just one additional year, a direct two-year comparison between the convertible bond and its higher-risk common stock becomes:

	Stock Price Change in 24 Months		
	−50 Percent	*0 Percent*	*+100 Percent*
Common stock total return	−50%	0%	+100%
Convertible bond total return	+ 2%	+22%	+100%

Which investor would you rather be? As surprising as it may seem, I must state unequivocally that practically all individual investors purchasing common stocks *are unaware that convertible bonds even exist!*

Exhibit 5–3. A typical new-issue convertible bond: National Medical Enterprises 8s of 2008

This announcement is under no circumstances to be construed as an offer to sell or as a solicitation of an offer to buy any of these securities. The offering is made only by the Prospectus.

NEW ISSUE

April 7, 1983

$200,000,000

National Medical Enterprises, Inc.

8% Convertible Subordinated Debentures due 2008

Price 100%

(Plus accrued interest from date of delivery, if any.)

Copies of the Prospectus may be obtained in any State in which this announcement is circulated from only such of the undersigned or other dealers or brokers as may lawfully offer these securities in such State.

Merrill Lynch White Weld Capital Markets Group
Merrill Lynch, Pierce, Fenner & Smith Incorporated

Bear, Stearns & Co. — The First Boston Corporation — Blyth Eastman Paine Webber Incorporated — Alex. Brown & Sons

Dillon, Read & Co. Inc. — Donaldson, Lufkin & Jenrette Securities Corporation — Drexel Burnham Lambert Incorporated — Hambrecht & Quist Incorporated

E. F. Hutton & Company Inc. — Kidder, Peabody & Co. Incorporated — Lazard Frères & Co. — Prudential-Bache Securities

L. F. Rothschild, Unterberg, Towbin — Salomon Brothers Inc — Shearson/American Express Inc.

Smith Barney, Harris Upham & Co. Incorporated — Warburg Paribas Becker A. G. Becker — Wertheim & Co., Inc. — Dean Witter Reynolds Inc.

Advest, Inc. — A. G. Edwards & Sons, Inc. — Oppenheimer & Co., Inc. — Thomson McKinnon Securities Inc.

Robert W. Baird & Co. Incorporated — Basle Securities Corporation — Bateman Eichler, Hill Richards Incorporated — William Blair & Company

Blunt Ellis & Loewi Incorporated — J. C. Bradford & Co. — Dain Bosworth Incorporated — F. Eberstadt & Co., Inc. — First of Michigan Corporation

Janney Montgomery Scott Inc. — Ladenburg, Thalmann & Co. Inc. — Cyrus J. Lawrence Incorporated — McDonald & Company

Montgomery Securities — Moseley, Hallgarten, Estabrook & Weeden Inc. — Piper, Jaffray & Hopwood Incorporated

Prescott, Ball & Turben, Inc. — Robinson Humphrey/American Express Inc — Rotan Mosle Inc.

Wheat, First Securities, Inc. — Sanford C. Bernstein & Co., Inc. — Birr, Wilson & Co., Inc. — Cowen & Co.

Crowell, Weedon & Co. — Davis, Skaggs & Co., Inc. — Laidlaw Adams & Peck Inc. — Legg Mason Wood Walker Incorporated

Morgan, Olmstead, Kennedy & Gardner Incorporated — Neuberger & Berman — Seidler Amdec Securities Inc.

Stephens Inc. — Sutro & Co. Incorporated — Underwood, Neuhaus & Co. Incorporated

NATIONAL MEDICAL ENTERPRISES, A TYPICAL NEW-ISSUE CONVERTIBLE

On April 7, 1983, a tombstone advertisement (Exhibit 5–3) announced the $200 million offering of a new convertible bond, the 8s of 2008 issued by National Medical Enterprises (NME). As other companies in the rapidly growing medical services industry, NME frequently uses convertible bonds to raise capital. They had two older issues outstanding at the time: $85 million of their 9s of 2006 and $124 million of their 12.625s of 2001. The new $200 million issue was quickly sold out to

Table 5–3. National Medical Enterprises' convertible bonds

	New Issue 8s of 2008	*Older Issue 12.625s of 2001*
Fundamental and technical data		
Common stock price	$33.25	
Common stock yield	1.5%	
Standard & Poor's stock ranking	A	
Value Line's performance rank	1	
Convertible's equity characteristics		
Convertible price	100	115
Conversion ratio	23.70	28.86
Conversion value	$787	$960
Conversion premium	27.1%	19.8%
Current yield	8.0%	11.0%
Yield advantage	6.5%	9.5%
Break-even time, years	3.3	1.7
Convertible's fixed-income characteristics		
Standard & Poor's bond rating	BBB	BBB
Straight bond equivalent yield	12.8%	12.8%
Investment value	$644	$988
Investment value premium	55.4%	16.4%

institutional money managers. My firm, which employs convertibles exclusively for our managed accounts, avoided the new issue. Why?

Table 5–3 compares the new 8s of 2008 and the older 12.625s of 2001 trading in the aftermarket. As shown by the comparison, the older issue provided substantial advantages; a lower conversion premium (19.8 versus 27.1 percent), a greater yield advantage (9.5 versus 6.5 percent), a shorter break-even time (1.7 versus 3.3 years), and a lower investment value premium (16.4 versus 55.4 percent). The older issue, the 12.625s of 2001, was clearly the superior choice. This was the NME convertible security my firm purchased for its clients.

The risk-reward calculations of Table 5–4 show both convertibles outperforming the traditional 50/50 combination of stock and straight bonds. The older issue, however, was superior to the new issue at all possible future stock prices. The convertible price curve for the older

Table 5–4. Risk-reward analysis: National Medical Enterprises' convertible bonds versus common stock at $33.25 and straight bonds at 12.8%

	Stock Price Change in 12 Months		
	−50 Percent	*0 Percent*	*+100 Percent*
Balanced approach			
Common stock	−48.5%	+ 1.5%	+101.5%
Straight bonds	+12.8	+12.8	+ 12.8
50% stock/50% bonds	−17.8%	+ 7.2%	+ 57.2%
8s of 2008 convertible bond			
Capital gain or loss	−20.7%	0%	+ 57.4%
Interest received	+ 8.0	+ 8.0	+ 8.0
Total return	−12.7%	+ 8.0%	+ 65.4%
Convertible advantage	+ 5.1%	+ 0.8%	+ 8.2%
12.625s of 2001 convertible bond			
Capital gain or loss	−13.0%	+ 0%	+ 67.0%
Interest received	+11.0	+11.0	+ 11.0
Total return	− 2.0%	+11.0%	+ 78.0%
Convertible advantage	+15.8%	+ 3.8%	+ 20.8%
Older issue advantage over new-issue convertible	+10.7%	+ 3.0%	+ 12.6%

12.625s of 2001 is presented as Exhibit 5–4. Exhibit 5–5 provides profit profiles for the 12.625s of 2001 and the 50/50 balanced approach. Notice how similar these profit profiles are to those illustrating the undervalued High-Tech convertible advantages (Exhibit 5–2).

Exhibit 5–4. The convertible price curve: National Medical Enterprises 12.625s of 2001 (conversion ratio = 28.86 shares, straight bond equivalent yield = 12.8 percent)

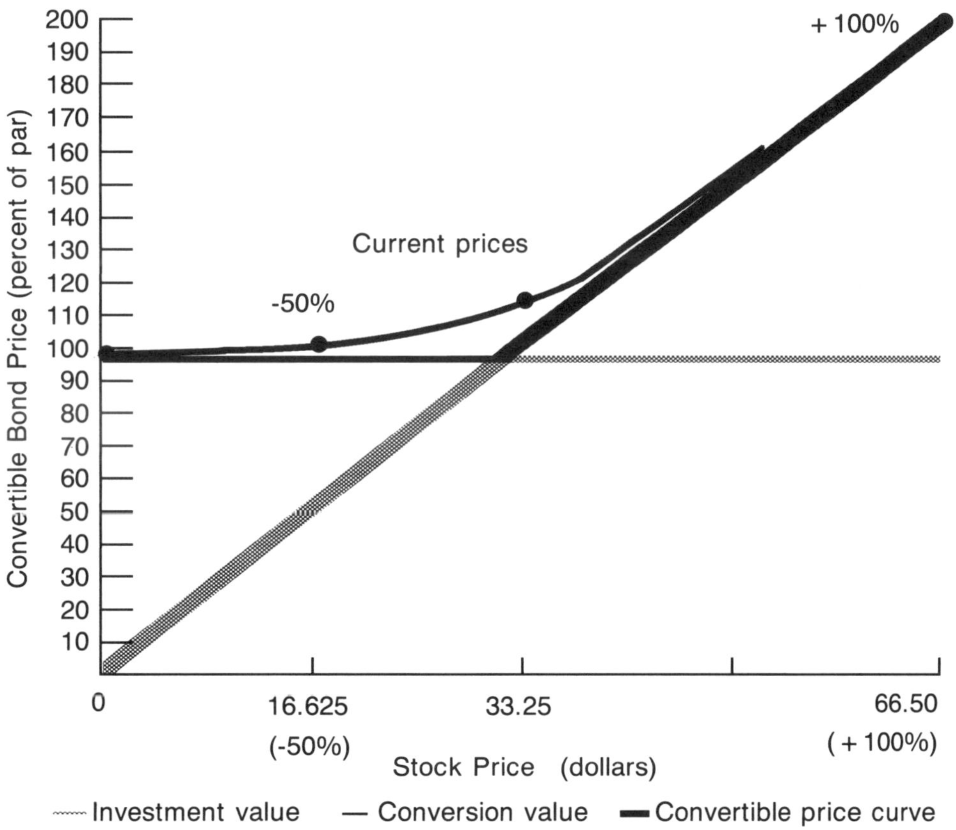

Exhibit 5–5. Profit profiles: National Medical Enterprises 12.625s of 2001 versus the balanced approach

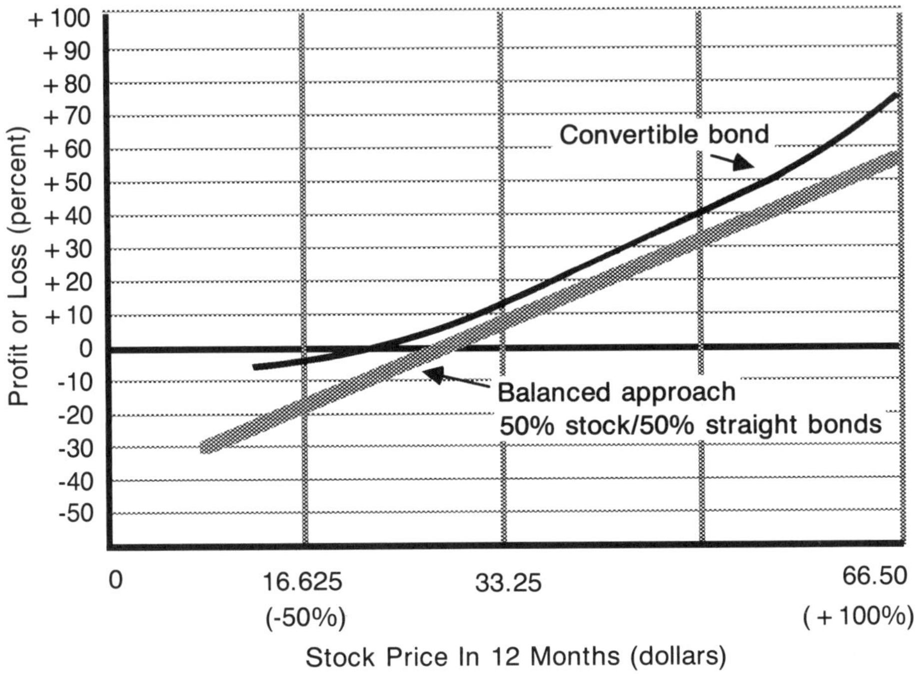

THE NATIONAL MEDICAL CONVERTIBLES ONE YEAR LATER

The NME bonds are an excellent example since it is hard to find two convertible bonds in the same company, especially where one is clearly superior to the other. My firm frequently uses the NME comparison at investment workshops to illustrate aftermarket bargains. The comparison also helps to emphasize the importance of controlling risk for long-term investment success. National Medical's common stock declined by 25 percent during the following 12 months, a year that also experienced rising interest rates, the worst combination of events for any investment program. Here are the prices for the three NME securities one year later compared to prices at the time the new convertible was issued:

	April 7, 1983	*April 7, 1984*
Common stock	$ 33.25	$ 25.00*
8s of 2008	100.00	82.50
12.625s of 2001	115.00	105.25

* The stock's $20 closing price was adjusted for a 5 to 4 split.

The total returns make very clear the older issue's advantage in the real world:

	Stock	*8s of 2008*	*12.625s of 2001*
Price change	−24.8%	−17.5%	− 8.5%
Dividends or interest	+ 1.5	+ 8.0	+11.0
Total return	−23.3%	− 9.5%	+ 2.5%

Remember, markets decline as often as they rise. Risk control is an important aspect of successful portfolio management.

SUBSTANTIALLY UNDERVALUED SECURITIES

While NME's new issue was undervalued, the older issue, trading in the aftermarket, must be termed *substantially undervalued.* The different strategies to be presented in the following chapters will be illustrated by substantially undervalued securities (e.g., the High-Tech convertible at 90 or real world examples such as the older National Medical Enterprises bond). These carefully selected investment opportunities enable investors to build low-risk/high-performance portfolios as illustrated in Chapter 2 by the convertible strategies line, repeated here as Exhibit 5–6.

As you can see by this graph, the convertible securities market offers opportunities ranging from very conservative deep-discount bonds to highly speculative warrants. The best strategy, or combination of strategies, will vary among investors depending on the personal risk-reward

Exhibit 5–6. The convertible strategies line compared to the capital market line

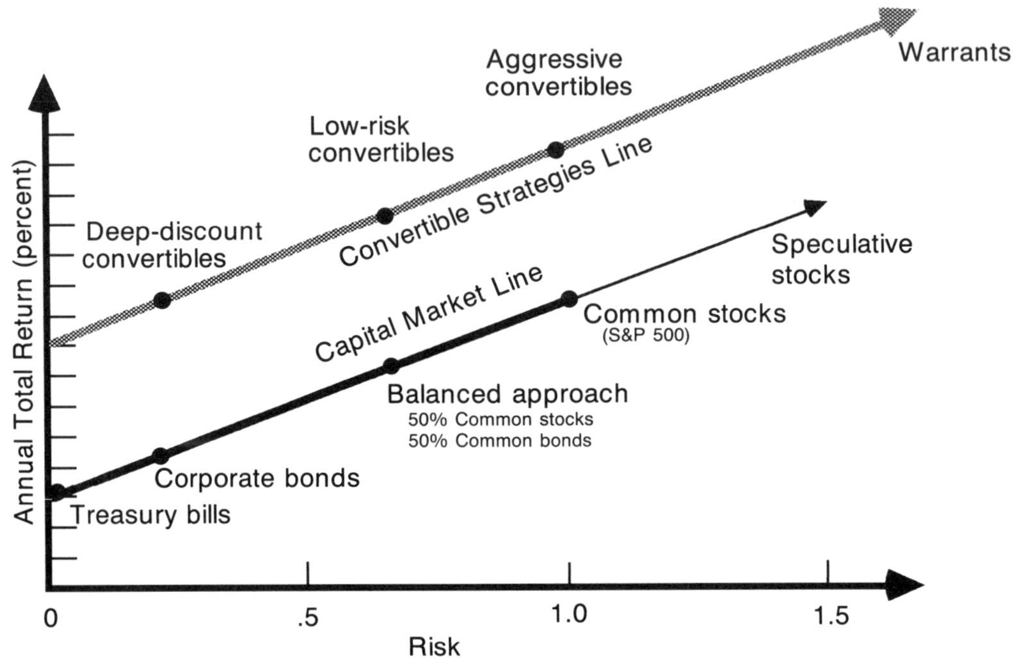

posture they choose to assume. All these strategies will be covered.

Be aware that investors who are knowledgeable about convertible strategies seldom, if ever, purchase traditional stocks or bonds. They know that far better alternatives exist in the convertible securities market. You may reach the same investment decision as you learn about real-world experiences in the following chapters.

CHAPTER 6

A Superior Alternative to Fixed-Income Investing

Once issued, a convertible bond's price will rise or fall in the trading aftermarket in tandem with its underlying common stock. By definition, any bond priced below par value is trading at a *discount.* The further it goes below par, the *deeper* the discount. This terminology applies to both convertible bonds and straight bonds, but not to preferreds.

Do discounted convertibles offer any advantages for the serious investor? Or are they inherently risky, as some presume, and hence poor investments? Let's examine our hypothetical High-Tech 10s of 2004 trading at a discounted price, resulting from a drop in the stock price from $20 down to $10 sometime after the bond was issued.

DISCOUNTED CONVERTIBLE BONDS

In chapter 5, I presented the undervalued High-Tech convertible trading at 90 when its common stock was at $20. The convertible price curve (Exhibit 5–1) predicted a bond price decline to 72 if the common dropped in half to $10. Since the bond was substantially undervalued at 90, we might expect that it would also be undervalued at 72, still trading on a price curve which passes through 90. The convertible price curve shown in Exhibit 6–1 repeats the previous curve and highlights current prices

Exhibit 6–1. The convertible price curve: High-Tech Industries 10s of 2004 trading at 72 (conversion ratio = 40 shares, straight bond equivalent yield = 16 percent)

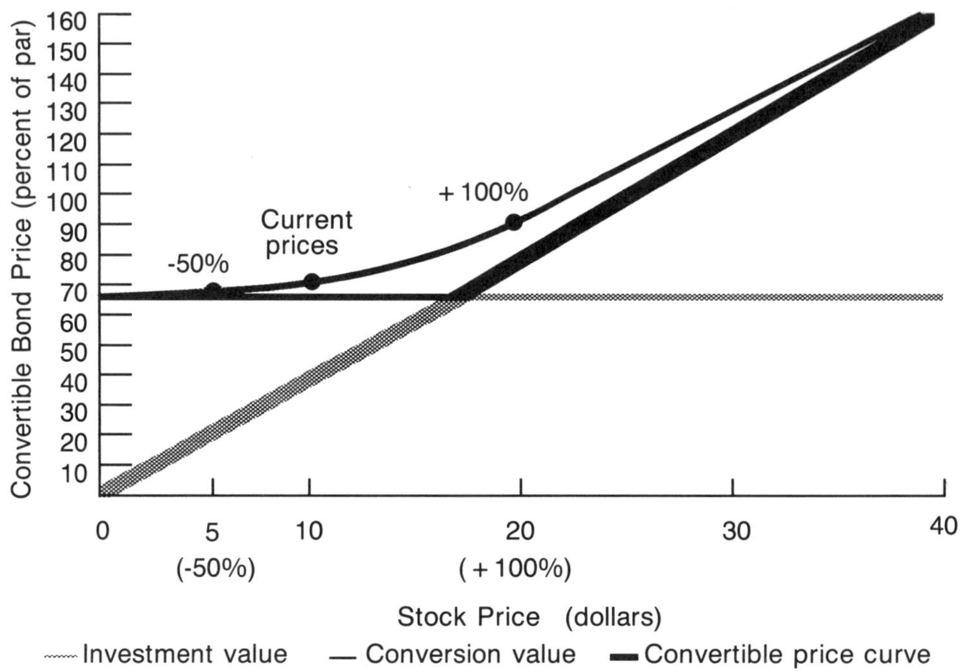

of 72 and \$10 along with future stock price changes of −50 percent and +100 percent from the \$10 level. I have assumed that if the common rebounded back to \$20, the convertible bond would again trade at 90. It could go back to its starting price of 100, or even higher, since the common would be back in favor after such a large advance. If the common declined by another 50 percent to \$5, we would anticipate a 5 point convertible price drop to 67, to within 2 points of its \$650 investment value floor. The High-Tech 10s of 2004 are obviously a much safer investment at 72 than at 90 or 100. This conclusion assumes, of course, that the stock declined in sympathy with the overall market, not because of deteriorating company fundamentals.

Table 6–1 presents a risk-reward analysis for the discounted High-Tech convertible compared to a 20/80 stock/bond portfolio. I chose the 20/80 combination instead of the 50/50 balanced approach I used

Table 6–1. Risk-reward analysis: High-Tech Industries 10s of 2004 at 72 versus common stock at $10 and straight bonds at 16 percent.

	Stock Price Change in 12 Months		
	−50 Percent	*0 Percent*	*+100 Percent*
Stock/straight bonds			
Common stock	−50%	0%	+100%
Straight bonds	+16	+16	+ 16
20% stock/80% bonds*	+ 3%	+13%	+ 33%
Convertible bond			
Capital gain or loss	− 7%	0%	+ 25%
Interest received	+14	+14	+ 14
Total return	+ 7%	+14%	+ 39%
Convertible advantage	+ 4%	+ 1%	+ 6%

* For a 20/80 stock/bond combination, the returns are weighted 20 percent for the stock performance and 80 percent for the bond performance. That is, for a 50 percent stock decline:

$$.20 \times -50\% = -10.0\%$$
$$.80 \times +16\% = +12.8$$
$$\text{total return} = +\ 2.8\% \text{ or } 3\% \text{ rounded}$$

earlier because at 72, the convertible bond will trade more as fixed-income than equity. Remember, to determine whether a convertible is undervalued you must compare it with traditional securities of the same company using a combination appropriate for the analysis.

As demonstrated by the risk-reward calculations, the convertible, having a 13.9 percent current yield (14.3 percent yield to maturity), offers greater downside protection (+7 versus +3 percent for a 50 percent stock decline) and greater upside opportunity (+39 versus +33 percent for a 100 percent stock advance). These are significant benefits for investors seeking income and safety.

DISCOUNT CONVERTIBLES VERSUS THE CAPITAL MARKET LINE

The convertible strategies line of Exhibit 6–2 highlights the risk-reward characteristics for undervalued discount convertibles in comparison to

Exhibit 6–2. Undervalued discount-convertible bonds compared to the capital market line

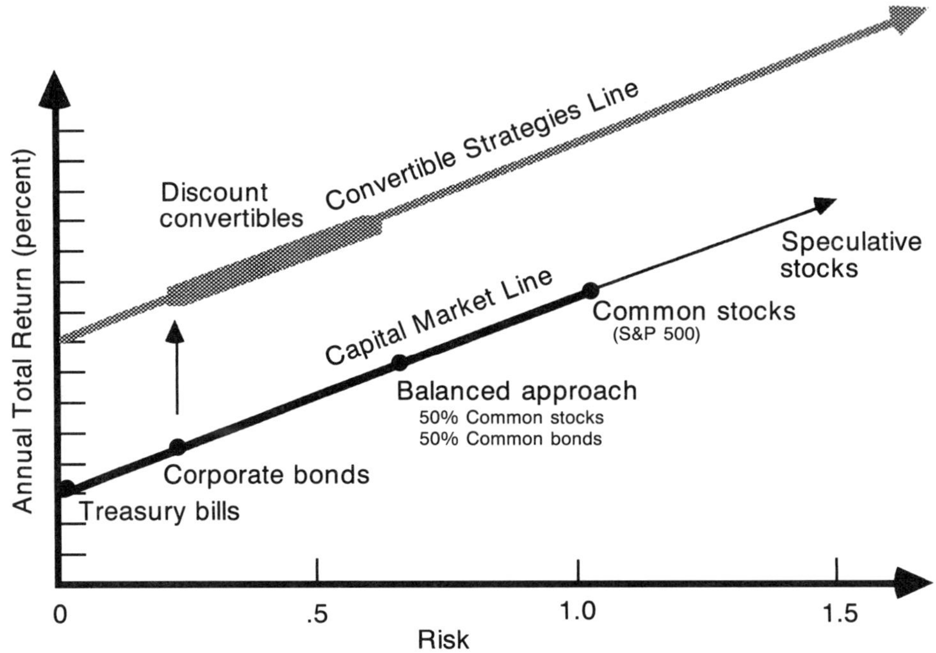

conventional stocks, bonds, and money market instruments. Their risk level is shown as a range on the convertible strategies line since not all discount convertibles are alike.

The lower area of the range is representative of *diversified portfolios* containing high-quality convertibles trading near their investment floors. Here, we may make a direct risk-reward comparison with high-quality straight bonds. Both risk and opportunity increase as convertibles are chosen further above their investment values and as quality ratings are lowered.

As with the capital market line, let me stress again that the convertible strategies line represents *broadly diversified* portfolios. The risk level for any single security would be much higher than the line suggests, without a corresponding increase in reward.

HISTORICAL PERFORMANCE DATA

Although a substantial amount of research on discounted straight bonds has accumulated over the years, the number of studies on discount convertibles is not as large. However, two of these studies are directly related to our High-Tech example.

In a paper published in *The Journal of Portfolio Management* (Spring 1977), W. Bradford Cornell presented a study for the period from 1964 through 1976. Contradicting modern portfolio theory, which states that all securities (including convertibles) are efficiently priced, Cornell's study offered evidence that discounted convertibles are *underpriced.* The explanation, he believed, is the institutional money managers' haste to sell convertible bonds when they drop well below par, especially when a company falls on hard times. Insufficient demand by individual investors to absorb the increased supply may then cause bond prices to fall below predictable levels. His conclusion is consistent with my earlier statement: Superior alternatives to traditional investing can only be those which large institutional portfolios cannot accommodate. The times when institutions are selling should provide even better opportunities for smaller investors!

A later and more extensive study was conducted at the University of Iowa. Richard A. Stevenson, Professor of Finance, also summarized his results in *The Journal of Portfolio Management* (Summer 1982). The study covered the ten year period from 1970 through 1979. It included all discounted convertible bonds trading on the New York and American Exchanges that were rated CCC or higher in quality, had a remaining life of more than ten years, and an issue size of at least $10 million. Based on its market price (not yield), each bond was arbitrarily placed into one of four categories—discount, deep discount, very deep discount, or extremely deep discount:

Discount Category	*Bond Price 1970–73*	*Bond Price 1974–79*
Discount	$701–$999	$651–$999
Deep discount	$561–$700	$521–$650
Very deep discount	$421–$560	$391–$520
Extremely deep discount	$420 or less	$390 or less

Table 6–2 summarizes the study's results. Discounted convertible bonds outperformed market indexes by a wide margin (an 11.0 percent annualized rate of return versus only 5.9 percent for the Standard & Poor's 500 stock index and 6.1 percent for the Salomon Brothers bond index). The study also demonstrated that risk, as measured by variability of return from year to year, was lower for discounted convertibles than for the market indexes.

Table 6–2 also shows that returns increased as the convertibles became less attractive to institutional money managers—poorer quality issues outperformed those having higher quality, smaller issues outperformed

Table 6–2. The University of Iowa study of discounted convertible bonds

	*Average Annual Return**	*10-Year Annualized Return†*
All discounted convertible bonds	+12.2%	+11.0%
By Standard & Poor's rating		
BBB or higher	+10.1	+ 9.5
BB	+11.4	+10.3
B	+12.9	+11.6
CCC	+13.9	+11.9
By issue size		
More than $50 million	+ 9.7	+ 8.3
$50 million or less	+12.6	+11.5
By exchange where listed		
New York Exchange	+12.2	+11.0
American Exchange	+13.5	+11.9
By degree of discount		
Discount (excluding 1970)	+ 9.8	—
Deep discount	+10.8	+ 9.8
Very deep discount	+12.8	+11.3
Extremely deep discount	+29.1	+25.3
Market indexes		
Standard & Poor's 500 stock index	+ 7.5	+ 5.9
Salomon Brothers bond index	+ 6.5	+ 6.1

* Arithmetic mean.
† Geometric mean.

larger issues, American Exchange issues outperformed those trading on the New York Exchange, and bonds having deeper discounts outperformed those with smaller discounts.

In its review of Professor Stevenson's research, *Market Logic* (3471 North Federal Highway, Fort Lauderdale, FL 33306), an advisory letter which searches out undervalued investment opportunities, reached these conclusions:

> First, investors desiring to maximize return for a given level of risk would do well to consider deep-discount convertible securities. Because they include some relatively troubled companies, however, they do entail greater risk. Thus, investment in one, or a tiny handful, of such securities could produce losses. Sufficient diversification can significantly reduce this risk.
>
> Second, any time you consider the purchase of a common stock, check first to determine whether a convertible security exists for that company. The lesson from the Stevenson research is that such convertibles, especially if they sell at relatively deep discounts from par value, should provide superior returns.

MY FAVORITE DEEP-DISCOUNT CONVERTIBLE

Although I have never managed a separate portfolio of discounted convertible bonds, I have used them extensively in conjunction with other convertible investment strategies. Following is an example illustrated in my book *How the Experts Beat the Market* (Dow Jones-Irwin, 1976).

In early 1975, the common stock of troubled Pan American World Airways was trading on the New York Stock Exchange near its all-time low at $2. I am sure most stock buyers were totally unaware of the availability of an attractive convertible alternative, the Pan American 7.5s of 1998. Exchangeable for 143 shares and trading at 30, the convertible was only slightly above its $286 conversion value. The stock and bond markets both believed that Pan Am was heading quickly towards bankruptcy.

As an alternative to its underlying common stock, the 7.5s of 1998 offered about the same capital gains potential if its common recovered. In addition, the bond provided a 25 percent current yield, compared to zero return for the nondividend-paying common. The common stock buyers simply overlooked an opportunity to increase their return on investment by 25 percent per year while reducing the risk they were willing to assume!

Those who purchased Pan American common at $2 in early 1975 and held it until its recovery to $9 in late 1983, where it was trading when the bond was called, were probably very pleased with their investment foresight. The nondividend-paying stock appreciated 350 percent in about nine years. However, those who bought the bonds at 30 would have received a 550 percent total return (330 percent capital appreciation from 30 to 129 plus income at 220 percent). Extremely undervalued situations such as the Pan Am deep-discount bonds occur on occasion. Conventional money ignores these opportunities—smart money capitalizes on them.

RECENT OPPORTUNITIES

Tables 6–3 and 6–4 list discounted convertible bonds traded on the New York and American Exchanges as of May 31, 1984. My selection criteria were similar to Stevenson's, though I modified them to reflect both the

Table 6–3. Discounted convertible bonds rated BBB or higher, May 31, 1984

Company Name	*Bond Description*	*Bond Price*	*Stock Price*	*Conversion Premium*	*Yield to Maturity*
Bally Manufacturing	10.00 –06	84.62	19.00	46	11.9
BankAmerica Realty	9.50 –08	93.25	25.25	14	10.2
Becton Dickinson	5.00 –89	76.00	32.62	51	10.9
Becton Dickinson[1]	10.75 –06	87.50	32.62	61	12.4
Big Three Industries	8.50 –06	77.50	21.50	57	11.2
Burlington Industries	8.75 –08	76.75	25.00	49	11.6
Cessna Aircraft	8.00 –08	79.00	17.75	45	10.1
Chase Manhattan	6.50 –96	72.00	39.50	5	10.6
Dana	5.875–06	58.38	22.25	32	10.8
Dominion Resources[2]	3.625–85	87.00	21.75	26	11.3
ENSERCH	10.00 –01	95.00	20.75	31	10.6
GATX[3]	5.75 –99	61.50	27.38	35	11.1

Table 6–3. (*Cont.*)

Company Name	*Bond Description*	*Bond Price*	*Stock Price*	*Conversion Premium*	*Yield to Maturity*
Great Western Financial	8.875–07	79.00	16.88	43	11.4
Greyhound[4]	6.00 –86	84.50	21.88	78	14.6
GTE	10.50 –07	98.00	36.25	24	10.7
InterFirst	7.75 –05	62.00	11.75	36	12.5
MAPCO	10.00 –05	87.00	28.25	41	11.6
McKesson	9.75 –06	93.00	33.38	22	10.5
MidCon	10.25 –09	98.25	34.50	20	10.4
Mobile[5]	10.50 –08	92.00	26.25	40	11.4
Norton Co.	9.50 –03	90.00	35.88	40	10.5
Paine Weber	8.25 –08	78.00	28.25	46	10.8
Pulte Home[6]	8.50 –08	79.50	12.25	54	10.9
Reynolds Industries[7]	10.00 –09	95.50	57.62	24	10.5
Tidewater	7.75 –05	69.00	22.62	96	11.7
Tracor	9.00 –07	90.50	21.00	31	10.0
Trinity Industries[8]	10.00 –06	95.00	16.75	53	10.5
U.S. Steel	5.75 –01	58.00	26.25	39	11.3
United Telecommun.[9]	5.00 –93	66.50	18.25	2	11.0
Wang Labs	7.75 –08	76.25	24.38	63	10.4
Xerox	6.00 –95	67.50	37.25	67	11.0
Averages (31 positions)				41	11.1

[1] Bond trades as Sun Co.
[2] Bond trades as Virginia Electric & Power.
[3] Bond trades as General American Transportation.
[4] Bond trades as Greyhound Computer.
[5] Bond trades as InterNorth.
[6] Bond trades as Pulte Home Credit.
[7] Bond trades as General Cinema.
[8] Bond trades as Trinity Industries Leasing.
[9] Bond trades as United Utilities.
Source: Standard & Poor's bond guide, June 1984.

higher interest rate environment prevailing in 1984 and certain other factors I thought relevant. I set the minimum yield to maturity for the higher-quality bonds of Table 6–3 (rated BBB or higher) at 10 percent. I choose 12 percent minimum for the low-quality issues of Table 6–4 (BB, B, and CCC). These percentages compare with straight bond yields ranging from 14 percent to 17 percent at the time (AA to CCC). In

Table 6–4. Discounted convertible bonds rated BB, B or CCC, May 31, 1984

Company Name	*Bond Description*	*Bond Price*	*Stock Price*	*Conversion Premium*	*Yield to Maturity*
Advest Group	9.00 –08	73.75	8.75	53	12.4
American Motors	6.00 –88	78.00	4.25	50	12.7
Anthony Industries	11.25 –00	88.50	11.25	42	12.9
Beefsteak Charlie's	13.00 –97	79.00	3.25	46	17.0
Bowmar Instrument	13.50 –95	86.50	3.62	84	16.1
Brown & Sharpe Mfg.	9.25 –05	70.00	14.88	65	13.5
Comdisco	8.00 –03	60.75	12.25	81	13.9
Crystal Oil	11.375–00	77.00	10.00	56	15.2
Delmed	10.50 –02	60.38	5.12	59	17.9
Diagnostic/Retrieval	8.50 –98	69.00	6.88	50	13.4
Eastern Air Lines	11.75 –05	68.00	4.75	86	17.5
Foothill Group	9.50 –03	76.00	4.75	44	12.9
Frontier Holdings	10.00 –07	71.50	12.00	53	14.2
Pacific Scientific	7.75 –03	60.00	12.62	80	13.7
Pan American	5.25 –89	61.25	5.25	92	17.7
Punta Gorda Isles	6.00 –92	55.00	7.00	53	16.3
Realty Income Trust	8.00 –91	80.00	7.00	89	12.1
Republic Airlines	10.125–07	58.00	3.75	55	17.6
Safeguard Bus. Systs.[1]	12.00 –96	79.00	15.75	52	15.9
Tacoma Boatbuilding	10.75 –01	81.00	8.00	39	13.6
Texas Air	8.375–00	60.00	5.75	77	15.0
Texscan	8.50 –03	72.00	12.38	75	12.3
Western Air Lines	5.25 –93	58.75	3.00	27	13.4
Western Air Lines	14.00 –98	90.00	3.00	55	15.7
Western Union	5.25 –97	51.00	23.88	41	13.1
Averages (25 positions)				60	14.6

[1] Bond trades as Safeguard Scientifics.
Source: Standard & Poor's bond guide, June 1984.

addition, I limited my selections to bonds having conversion premiums below 100 percent. I felt that convertibles trading at higher premiums lacked sufficient responsiveness to their common stock movements and thus were trading essentially as discounted straight bonds. The other departure from Stevenson was the bond's remaining life to maturity date.

He included only bonds having more than ten years life, while I did not make a maturity-date distinction. I personally favor the shortest-term bond when given a choice; an approaching maturity date will propel the bond's price toward par.

As shown by Tables 6–3 and 6–4, 56 situations met my selection criteria (over 400 discounted convertibles were available). Since new candidates would certainly be added to the lists from time to time, it would seem that more than ample opportunities existed for establishing broadly diversified portfolios.

Additional departures from Stevenson's qualifying criteria could be to consider minimum issue sizes smaller than $10 million and bonds traded over-the-counter. If smaller issue or thinly traded OTC bonds become attractive purchase candidates, why not consider them? The only difficulty might be in obtaining a fair price if the bonds had to be sold quickly at a later time. Assuming the investor's intention is to hold for the long term, there should be no liquidity problems. Investors should look at discount bonds only as long-term acquisitions. They are not trading vehicles. At maturity, the company will redeem them for cash. In the meantime, if the underlying common stock experiences a substantial advance (as did Pan American) the thinly-traded bonds could be exchanged for stock and the stock sold.

Notice that bond coupons ranged from only 3.625 percent up to 14.0 percent. Both extremes were represented by bonds in the same company, Western Air Lines (WAL); let's compare their pluses and minuses. The WAL 5.25s of 1993 at 58.75 provide a relatively low 8.9 percent current yield. A large part of its 13.4 percent yield to maturity is the annual price appreciation the bond will experience as it rises from below 60 to par value over the next few years. Investors wanting higher current income would choose WAL's 14s of 1998 which offers a 15.6 percent current yield at a price of 90. For investors concerned about reducing their income tax liabilities, the low-coupon bond might be the better choice. Under current tax law for bonds issued prior to June 1984, its built-in price appreciation will be taxed later and will be subject to a tax rate of only 40 percent of that applying to ordinary income. Therefore, individual investors would probably prefer the 5.25s of 1993 while tax-exempt (or tax-deferred) investors would choose the higher-yielding 14s of 1998.

As Cornell and Stevenson, I did not limit Tables 6–3 and 6–4 to those convertibles I calculated to be undervalued as in the High-Tech example.

Detailed analyses of all convertible bonds on the lists did show that many offered attractive risk-reward characteristics similar to those of the High-Tech 10s of 2004 trading at 72. However, a surprising number were actually overpriced relative to stock/straight-bond combinations, especially low-coupon issues in name companies such as U.S. Steel and Xerox. This further indicates that the best opportunities continue to be with the lower-quality convertibles. It also reinforces the importance of preparing risk-reward calculations before making any convertible bond purchase.

I heartily agree with *Market Logic* and others who advocate the use of discounted convertible bonds. This is one of several inefficiently priced market sectors you will learn about in this book. This niche is particularly suited for long-term investors seeking high current income plus modest capital appreciation. However, since the best selection candidates are the lower-quality issues, be aware that some may wind up in default. Therefore, I strongly urge a higher degree of portfolio diversification than you would normally employ for other investment strategies; at least 20 or more different issues for all but the most aggressive investors. Diversification improves the odds that any inherently sound investment strategy will be successful.

Let me add that I don't believe fundamental analysis of the securities under consideration will be of much value in the selection process. As Pan American in 1975, company prospects will likely range from bad to horrible. Technical analysis may also be futile, since most technical systems focus on the best performing companies, not the worst. The proper approach, I believe, is careful selection based on mathematical relationships, as I have illustrated, coupled with maximum portfolio diversification.

However, deep-discount convertibles are clearly best for investors who want to maximize current income. We must look at other undervalued convertibles if we wish more capital appreciation. Let us then move up the convertible strategies line to the region of low-risk convertibles.

CHAPTER 7

A Superior Alternative to Balanced Portfolios

Most investors are seeking more than current income from their investments. They also want their investments to increase in value. While their capital is growing, they pay less in taxes on added wealth. Only then can they be sure of future income for retirement days.

The vast majority of investors seek their wealth with something akin to the balanced approach. They use stocks, bonds, and money market instruments in various combinations. Too few realize that undervalued *low-risk convertibles* are a superior alternative to these conservatively structured portfolios.

By my definition, the term *low-risk* describes a particular convertible security with inherent risk characteristics similar to those of a mix of *high-quality* stocks and bonds. If the convertibles are also undervalued, a diversified portfolio of these attractive securities can be expected to outperform traditional stocks and bonds. They are then a low-risk/high-return strategy for investors seeking income and capital gains.

LOW-RISK CONVERTIBLES VERSUS THE CAPITAL MARKET LINE

Exhibit 7–1 compares risk-reward relationships for *undervalued* low-risk convertibles with conventional stocks, bonds, and Treasury bills. As with

Exhibit 7–1. Undervalued low-risk convertible bonds compared to the capital market line

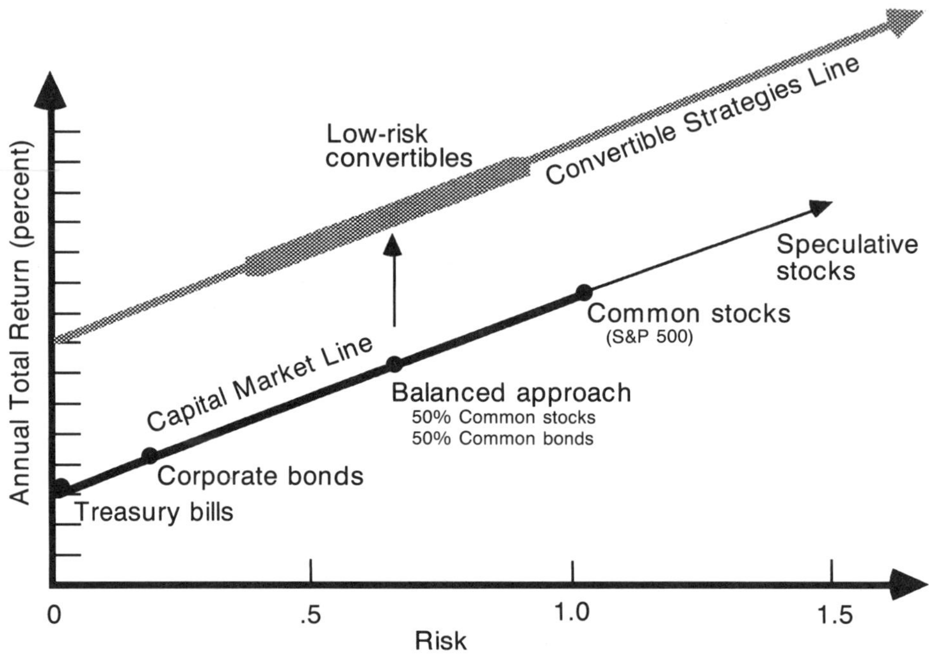

the discounted convertibles of Chapter 6, the risk level is illustrated by a range on the convertible strategies line, since no two convertibles are identical. Where might a particular issue fall within the range? There are four major factors to consider: the quality of the convertible's underlying common stock (the company), its current yield, its price, and its remaining life to maturity.

The best low-risk convertibles are based on high-quality stocks. The indicators which best represent the high-quality sector of the stock market are Standard & Poor's 500 Stock Index and the Dow Jones Industrial Average. Every stock within the two groups may be evaluated by some type of quality measurement; I chose the widely used S&P earnings and dividend ranking system to construct Table 7–1.

As we should expect, most of the S&P 500 and DJIA stocks received B+ rankings (average) or higher. In the broader S&P, close examination shows the larger companies, having the greatest impact on this market value-weighted index, generally ranked above average (A–, A, or A+).

Table 7–1. The S&P 500 Stock Index and the Dow Jones Industrial Average

S&P Rank	*Quality Level*	*Number of Stocks* *S&P 500*	*DJIA*
A+	highest	88	8
A	high	105	5
A−	above average	97	6
B+	average	95	2
B	below average	53	5
B−	lower	27	3
C	lowest	16	1
D	in reorganization	0	0
NR	not rated	19	0
		500	30

It would seem logical, therefore, that stocks underlying low-risk convertibles should have a *minimum* S&P rank of B+. Thus, our first criterion for labeling a convertible as low-risk is a B+ or higher Standard & Poor's ranking for its underlying common—the higher the ranking, the lower the convertible's risk. A well diversified low-risk convertible securities portfolio should reflect the high-quality standards of the index itself.

The best low-risk convertibles also offer good yields. The typical new, high-quality convertible bond issued in 1983 offered an 8.0 percent coupon (Table 3–3). Trading at par, these new-issue convertibles would be termed low-risk. If their prices declined later, we would relabel them as deep-discounts (Chapter 6) at some lower price level. On the upside, as a convertible's price advances above par, it takes on more of the risk characteristics of its common stock. At some higher price level the convertible would be reassigned to a higher-risk category. While I have no hard and fast rules, a price range of 90 to 110 would probably be appropriate for calling high-quality 8.0 percent coupon bonds low-risk in 1983. (The range will shift with long-term interest rates.)

Previously issued convertibles may have substantially lower or higher coupons than our 8.0 percent example. Two convertibles which are exchangeable for G. D. Searle's common, for instance, have coupons of 4.50 and 5.25 percent. For a low-yielding bond, I look for a low-risk current price range of about 70 to 90. For coupons of 11 or 12 percent, the current range would be about 110 to 130. Again, I am not suggesting any hard and fast rules; remember, the higher the coupon, the lower the risk.

Remaining life to maturity is the other major factor used to identify a convertible bond's risk level. Since the investment floor rises to par value at maturity, even a low-coupon bond, trading modestly above par, could be labeled low-risk if it matures in just a few years. The Searle 5.25s of 1989, for example, would be termed low-risk when trading near par (instead of the 70 to 90 range).

I purposely omitted bond ratings from the four parameters. Since the primary consideration in bond ratings is the company's ability to meet its interest payment and redemption obligations, its rating is important when evaluating a straight bond. Rating services consider the same company-related factors when judging convertible bonds, but they do not take stock market risk into account. A convertible rated BBB when issued at par, for example, will probably still be rated BBB when later trading at 150 or 200; it might even be upgraded to a higher-quality rating if the stock's higher price reflects improved company fundamentals. Trading further above its investment floor, the convertible bond is obviously much riskier at higher prices than it was at par, regardless of the rating assigned by the services.

I have also seen instances where balanced-approach investors arbitrarily decide they will buy only bonds rated A or higher for the fixed-income portion of their portfolios (straight or convertibles). They may then turn around and purchase B ranked common stock for their portfolio's equity side in lieu of a much safer BBB convertible bond, more than likely a better alternative to their balanced approach. This narrow-sighted thinking is especially common among many institutional investors or their counselors, who believe they must place every strategy in *either* a fixed-income *or* an equity category; otherwise, it may be too "difficult" for them to evaluate their money manager's performance. I am not painting all institutional investors with a "broad brush" since a few are extremely sophisticated in their handling of convertibles.

Individual investors, however, should not burden themselves with misconceived portfolio restrictions. They should aggressively take advantage of undervalued convertible opportunities! This means building convertible-securities portfolios whose core holdings are high-quality, low-risk convertible bonds. An investor's major problem is finding and selecting specific issues and later deciding when to sell them.

BUILDING A LOW-RISK CONVERTIBLE SECURITIES PORTFOLIO

This chapter introduces the tools and buy/sell guidelines needed to build and manage a successful portfolio of low-risk convertible securities, the superior alternative to combination portfolios of high-quality stocks and bonds. Chapter 9 will provide the information you need to construct a convertible portfolio as a higher-return alternative to the stock market itself.

Portfolio Diversification

Most individual portfolios are inadequately diversified. They will therefore not perform as desired, relative to the markets. Owners of these poorly diversified portfolios are unable to evaluate them against meaningful standards; they never know whether performance (good or bad) is the result of their securities selection ability or plain luck. Other portfolios may attempt diversification through a large number of different issues, but include securities in closely related industries, thus defeating the purpose of diversification.

Proper diversification is an essential ingredient for any investment program which is to be measured against market indexes. For a portfolio of low-risk convertibles, I would recommend a minimum of 10 different issues in *unrelated* industries. Ten different issues, I repeat, is the *minimum,* and should be considered only by investors willing to accept the high probability that year-to-year results will depart from the performance of larger, well-diversified portfolios.

Bearing in mind the strong likelihood that attractive opportunities may fall within closely related industry groups, I prefer 20 or more positions and consider broad diversification to mean 30 to 40 issues. My experience has been that broadly diversified portfolios display fairly consistent performance and can usually be accurately compared with market indexes. However, even these larger portfolios may diverge from the markets over short periods of time, just as the DJIA of 30 stocks does not precisely track the S&P 500. The divergence between the two was especially pronounced a few years ago, when IBM was in the S&P but not the Dow; today, it is in both.

Most investors introduced to convertibles for the first time tend to think of this "newly discovered" strategy as a specialty area of the markets; typically, they give it a small portion of their capital for a year or so to see if it "works." This often means their convertible portfolio is underdiversified. If it performs below expectations, they tend to blame the "mystical" convertibles and not the poorly performing underlying common stocks which caused the portfolio to decline. Having formed an erroneous conclusion based upon too small a sample and insufficient time, they give up and retreat to traditional investment arenas. If they viewed convertible investing as the superior alternative it is, they would have committed the bulk, if not all of their investment capital to the strategy. Given proper diversification, they would probably have experienced satisfactory performance and decide to stay with it for the long term.

Remember, a portfolio of 20 low-risk convertible bonds, for example, *replaces* 20 different corporate bonds *and* 20 different common stocks. It is the equivalent to a combination portfolio containing 40 securities. Convertibles are not specialty instruments. They are *alternative investments!*

Stock Beta Ratings

A popular tool for identifying stock market risk is *beta:* a measure of the historical sensitivity of a stock's price movements to overall market fluctuations. For example, a beta of 1.50 indicates that a stock rose (or fell) in the past by 15 percent for each 10 percent rise (or fall) of the market as measured by a diversified index such as the S&P 500. A beta of .50 indicates that a stock is only half as risky (or profitable) as the market. Most betas will fall between .75 and 1.50; highly market-sensitive securities, such as brokerage firm stocks, may have betas as high as 2.0; some utility stocks are below .75.

Since beta includes dividends, it is not a precise measure of actual price movements. Nor is it an infallible predictor of future dividend-adjusted price changes. All beta figures should be treated, at best, as educated guesses about what might happen in the future. While any single beta could fail completely in forecasting future price movements, I agree with most professionals who believe that a diversified portfolio's beta average is a useful tool for estimating the portfolio's risk and opportunity relative to the overall market.

Low-risk convertibles *are an alternative* to the balanced approach and should be compared with a combination of stock and bond market indexes. The average beta for the underlying common stocks should be close to 1.0 for the convertible portfolio to be termed "low-risk." Portfolios having beta averages well above or below 1.0 belong in different categories.

Fundamental and Technical Analysis

Proponents of the efficient market concept advise that neither fundamental nor technical analysis will help investors gain an edge on the markets. Most money managers, such as my firm, disagree; we believe we have the expertise to identify undervalued opportunities.

As you saw in Chapters 5 and 6, convertible securities can be substantially undervalued even when assuming that their underlying common stocks are efficiently priced. If one can logically conclude that its common is undervalued as well, then the convertible should offer even greater opportunity than would normally be expected.

The key to building a convertible securities portfolio is first to identify the most attractive convertibles available in the marketplace, not the most attractive companies. Later, as the final step in the decision process, you may apply both fundamental and technical analysis to their common stocks. As a result, some of the convertible candidates will be rejected. Those who pick stocks first, and then check to see if there is an attractive convertible alternative, might as well forget about a convertible securities investment program.

Of the 500 plus convertibles that my firm continuously monitors, only 10 to 20 are attractive purchase candidates on a day-to-day basis. This represents only about one percent of the companies listed on the New York Stock Exchange. Investors who look at stocks first will then find that seeking attractive convertible securities is a highly discouraging endeavor. They may discover several modestly undervalued issues, but they will seldom find true bargains. Bargains are quickly snapped up by firms, such as my own, that can act immediately on favorable situations.

Research

The most important tool for successful investing in convertible securities is research—a systematic and thorough evaluation of all possible candidates needed to uncover the few that offer exceptional risk-reward characteristics. Other tools discussed in this chapter are important, but they are not nearly as crucial as finding the most attractive opportunities.

A convenient source of statistical data that includes conversion ratios and investment values is an absolute must. There are several brokerage firms and advisory services that provide important information. The best is *Value Line Convertibles*[1], published weekly. This service is used by most convertible specialists. *Value Line* includes not only necessary statistical data, but in-depth information on specific securities via footnotes, special bulletins, and individual company studies. Access to the service, or a low-cost trial subscription, should be obtained by any investor interested in executing the strategies presented in this book.

GUIDELINES FOR BUYING LOW-RISK CONVERTIBLES

Following are my basic guidelines for buying low-risk convertibles (bonds and preferreds) as an alternative to a traditional portfolio of common stock and corporate bonds.

1. Decide how much diversification you want. I suggest a minimum of 20 issues in diverse industries, with approximately equal dollars invested in each position. If you find two or more attractive situations in the same industry group, consider taking smaller positions in each. If you find more than 20 different candidates, do not hesitate to increase the total number since greater diversification assures more consistent performance, though it involves some extra bookkeeping and transaction costs.
2. Establish disciplined procedures for evaluating potential candidates and always prepare a risk-reward analysis; you are looking for truly undervalued opportunities, not the run-of-the-mill issue.
3. Check the common stocks underlying all convertible candidates for B+ or higher Standard & Poor's rankings.
4. Maintain the average current yield for your overall convertible portfolio comparable to new, high-quality issues being brought to the market—8.0 percent in 1983, for example.
5. Keep the average beta for the common stocks underlying the convertible securities portfolio at about 1.0.

6. Apply your own fundamental or technical analysis to the underlying common stocks or rely, as I do, on investment advisory services that are better equipped for the task. Remember, however, that this is the *last* step in the selection process. The best convertible candidates should be chosen first.

Table 7–2 presents a sample portfolio of 10 convertibles that, when available in June 1984, fitted the above purchase guidelines. The ten issues were selected from different industries and their underlying common stocks were all rated at average or above for year-ahead performance by *The Value Line Investment Survey* (not to be confused with *Value Line Convertibles*). The 9.0 percent current yield for the sample portfolio, compared to 8.0 percent for new issues in 1983, reflected the higher long-term interest rates prevailing in mid-1984. The convertibles offered about three-fourths the upside opportunity of their common stocks (+77 percent versus +100 percent) at only about half the risk (−23 percent versus −50 percent), plus a yield advantage of about 5 percent.

Table 7–2. Undervalued low-risk convertible bonds available in June 1984

				*Leverages**		
Company Name	*Bond Description*	*Bond Price*	*Current Yield*	*−50 Percent*	*+100 Percent*	*Stock Beta*
Allied Stores	9.50 -07	112	8.5	−26%	+86%	.80
American General	11.00 -07	123	8.9	−24	+82	.85
Amer. Medical Int'l.	9.50 -01	111	8.6	−23	+73	1.35
Barnett Banks of Fla.	12.25 -06	124	9.8	−21	+77	1.00
Celanese	9.75 -06	105	9.3	−24	+84	.90
Lomas & Nettleton	9.75 -08	104	9.4	−22	+75	1.05
MacMillan	8.75 -08	107	8.2	−26	+78	.85
Quaker State Oil	8.875-08	97	9.1	−22	+68	1.25
Research Cottrell	10.50 -06	113	9.3	−22	+70	1.15
SCOA Industries	10.00 -97	113	8.9	−24	+80	.90
Averages (10 positions)			9.0%	−23%	+77%	1.01

* The estimated percent change for the convertible for changes in the price of the underlying stock of −50 or +100 percent.

Source: Noddings, Calamos & Associates' research.

GUIDELINES FOR SELLING LOW-RISK CONVERTIBLES

Convertible portfolios require *active management* for maximum long-term performance. Convertibles are selected on the basis of common sense and risk-reward relationships and should be monitored along the same lines. When any one of the following conditions are met, the convertible should be sold and replaced with a new selection that meets the original buy criteria.

Convertible price advances. As the underlying common stock rises and the convertible trades well above par, take profits; the convertible no longer provides the downside safety originally sought. (Its current yield is down considerably and its yield to maturity is even lower.) By replacing that high-priced convertible with a security trading near par, you realize a profit and also protect the profit by again buying a convertible that meets the original selection guidelines. Not taking profits when a convertible advances to well above par is the same as changing your investment objective to the higher-risk posture of the stock market.

Convertible price declines. When the common stock drops, the convertible will lag behind as it approaches its investment value. The convertible has fulfilled its downside protection function. It has decreased less than the common and now takes on more of the risk-reward characteristics of a straight debt instrument. Because the conversion premium has increased, the convertible will now trail well behind its stock on any future price advance. Not selling a convertible when it is trading at a deep discount is the same as changing your investment objective to the lower-risk level of the fixed-income market.

Convertible loses its undervaluation. Any time a convertible loses the favorable risk-reward characteristics that made it an attractive purchase, it should be sold. We are working in an area where inefficiencies often develop. For no apparent reason, you may find the common going down and the convertible going up, or the convertible declining by less than would be expected. In either case, a new risk-reward analysis may indicate that the convertible is no longer undervalued. Take advantage of these market inefficiencies by replacing that convertible with a superior alternative if one is available.

A marginal convertible may be sold to take advantage of an exceptional alternative. Since you should continually keep your portfolio in positions that will participate in a market advance at low risk, a marginal convertible—one that has not quite reached a point where a sell is indicated—may be replaced with an exceptional alternative.

These basic guidelines provide a systematic framework for continually monitoring a low-risk convertible securities portfolio. They will allow you to maintain the most advantageous risk-reward posture for participation in an advancing market and for protection in a declining market. You will never become "married" to any security you own. It is one of the few sure ways I have ever seen that allows you to remove most emotions from investing while increasing the odds in your favor. Note that these sell guidelines specifically pertain to a low-risk portfolio. If your overall investment program includes other convertible strategies, such as the deep discounts of Chapter 6, it may not be necessary to sell as indicated; simply reassign the convertible to the appropriate strategy.

EXECUTING ORDERS FOR BUYING OR SELLING CONVERTIBLES

These guidelines should be carefully followed when placing buy or sell orders. Order execution for a convertible program is much more critical to your success than when purchasing stocks or bonds. Remember the convertible markets are not as liquid, so careful order execution can mean extra profits.

1. Select actively traded convertibles, having a large issue size outstanding and listed on the New York Stock Exchange, whenever possible.
2. Monitor both the convertible and its underlying stock prices prior to entering orders: A good "feel" for their related prices permits you to execute orders at favorable prices and will save you money, whether buying or selling.
3. Place orders through a brokerage firm that has skills in executing listed bond orders in the over-the-counter (off-board) market: Most listed bonds are more actively traded off-the-board than on the floor of the exchange.
4. Work with a stockbroker who has special training in evaluating convertibles and in executing orders: The broker's knowledge and skills are

much more critical to your investment success in this area than when buying or selling common stocks or straight bonds.

If you can follow all the guidelines offered in this chapter, you should be able to make investing in low-risk convertibles work for you. Remember that the keys to success are: prudent selection of the convertible issues, careful timing of transactions, and diligent maintenance of the low-risk character of your portfolio.

You can measure your success against various stock market and bond indexes, but such indexes are not strictly relevant to the convertible securities market. The Noddings-Calamos low-risk convertible bond index, to be presented in Chapter 8, is a first-of-its-kind indicator. It has tracked the performance of undervalued low-risk convertible securities since its inception in 1976; it can be very useful to the astute investor.

NOTES FOR CHAPTER 7

1. *Disclosure:* This author has no financial interest in *Value Line;* I believe their work to be worth the expense. Free brokerage publications on the subject are valuable, but convertible securities research by brokerage firms is incidental to their primary research activities involving common stocks. Their convertible expertise does not measure up to *Value Line's* high commitment to this sophisticated market niche. Available from Arnold Bernhard & Co., 711 Third Avenue, New York, N.Y. 10017, $295 per year.

CHAPTER 8

The Noddings-Calamos Low-Risk Convertible Bond Index

The problem of tracking convertible bond performance has existed as long as the bonds themselves. As convertibles have gained in popularity, it is only in the last decade that anyone has tried to put together a useful performance index for *undervalued* issues. This index is the Noddings-Calamos *low-risk* convertible bond index. The related Noddings-Calamos *aggressive* convertible bond index will be presented in Chapter 9.

I first presented the background for the Noddings-Calamos convertible indexes in my book, *The Investor's Guide to Convertible Bonds.*[1] That book discussed two detailed studies of the indexes, each intended to support favorable theories with actual market experiences. These studies covered the six year period from 1976 to 1981. Here, I update the data through mid-1984.

The Noddings-Calamos indexes are, unlike other indexes, based on actual purchases and sales. However, because our clients use a combination of different convertible strategies with the mix dependent on market opportunities, you should view the indexes as indicators of market opportunity at specified risk levels (the convertible strategies line); they are not "track records" of account performance.

CONSTRUCTION PARAMETERS

Account selection. In order to manage better the enormous task of data analysis, and to avoid complicating the results by using buy and sell decisions of clients managed under different investment objectives, we chose to calculate convertible bond performance using a single account on a quarterly basis. The one selected for each quarter's calculation was the largest and the most *diversified* under my firm's full management at the beginning of the quarter. We took on our first institutional client in mid-1981. This larger client was not appropriate for the index, however, since it used a limited strategy which did not encompass all issues available in the low-risk sector of the convertible securities market. Thus, it has never been a part of this index. Five different accounts have been used for the index over the 8.5 years.

Security selection. Our clients use varying convertible strategies; thus not all issues held by the five accounts were used to calculate the index. The convertibles selected had underlying common stocks ranked B+ or higher by Standard & Poor's (Chapter 7). Most were listed on the New York Stock Exchange, but occasionally a high-risk American Exchange or over-the-counter company would receive a B+ rating. Beginning in 1984, we improved our selection criteria by excluding stocks not listed on the New York Stock Exchange. We implemented this refinement to achieve our goal, a low-risk convertible index truly reflective of the high-quality sector of the market.

Also in 1984, the rapidly expanding convertible bond market, which provided opportunities for greater portfolio diversification, allowed us to delete convertible preferreds from the index. This second improvement helped elevate the index to today's higher level of quality. Table 8–1 lists the 27 different convertible bonds employed in the index as of June 30, 1984.

Weighting. We give equal representation in each quarter's index to each convertible security, since the actual dollar value of positions held in the client portfolios may vary. A given quarter's gain or loss can thus be readily computed using percentage price changes plus income earned. Equal weighting also eliminates the possible distortions that larger positions might have on the results.

Table 8–1. The Noddings-Calamos low-risk convertible bond index, positions held on June 30, 1984

Company Name	*Bond Description*	*Bond Price*	*Current Yield*	*Stock Beta*	*S&P Stock Rank*
Allied Corp.[1]	7.75 –05	92.00	8.4%	1.15	A–
Allied Stores	9.50 –07	112.50	8.4	.80	A+
American General	11.00 –07	123.50	8.9	.85	A
American Medical Int'l.	13.00 –01	147.00	8.8	1.35	A
Barnett Banks of Florida	12.25 –06	124.00	9.9	1.00	A
Burlington Industries	5.00 –91	79.12	6.3	.95	B+
Celanese Corp.	9.75 –06	104.00	9.4	.90	B+
Chase Manhattan	6.50 –96	70.50	9.2	.95	A–
GTE Corp.	10.50 –07	100.00	10.0	.85	A+
Inexco Oil	8.50 –00	74.75	11.4	1.45	B+
Kaneb Services[2]	8.75 –08	89.00	9.8	1.25	A–
Leggett & Platt	8.125–01	94.00	8.6	.90	A–
McKesson Corp.	9.75 –06	95.75	10.2	.80	A
Merrill Lynch	8.875–07	102.00	8.7	1.75	B+
Nat'l. Convenience Stores	9.00 –08	88.00	10.2	1.05	A–
Nat'l. Medical Enterprises	12.625–01	103.50	12.2	1.40	A
Newell Cos.	8.75 –03	85.50	10.2	.85	A–
Paine Webber[3]	8.00 –05	90.50	8.8	2.00	B+
Pogo Producing	8.00 –05	72.50	11.0	1.15	B+
Quaker State Oil	8.875–08	96.00	9.2	1.25	B+
Reynolds Industries[4]	10.00 –08	107.50	9.3	.95	A+
SCOA Industries	10.00 –07	118.50	8.4	.90	A+
Seagram Co. Ltd.	8.25 –08	101.75	8.1	1.05	A
Southwest Airlines	10.00 –07	121.00	8.3	1.10	B+
United Telecommun.[5]	5.00 –93	69.00	7.2	.90	A+
Viacom International	9.25 –07	105.00	8.8	1.30	B+
Walter, Jim Corp.	5.75 –91	82.50	7.0	1.10	B+
Averages (27 positions)			9.1%	1.11	

[1] Bond trades as Textron.
[2] Bond trades as Moran Energy.
[3] Bond trades as CIGNA Corp.
[4] Bond trades as General Cinema.
[5] Bond trades as United Utilities.

Minimum position size. We establish minimum position sizes to assure fair results since some convertibles are not actively traded. For example, if the minimum size chosen is 50 bonds, and only 10 are purchased at our carefully established price, that particular issue is excluded from the index. (Its inclusion would cause an upward performance bias, since an immediate price rise prevents us from completing our desired position size.)

Pricing. Actual purchase and sale prices are used to calculate results. Others, who base their hypothetical performance records on last-traded exchange prices, wind up with totally misleading results. There is always a price spread for any security which can distort the results. In addition, a convertible might not trade for several days, while its stock may be making a major price move. The last traded price can quickly become meaningless; I have seen bonds whose last reported prices were 20 points or more away from their true markets.

Management and trading expenses. All convertible programs must be actively managed to maintain the portfolio's desired risk-reward characteristics and to achieve maximum profits over a market cycle. Therefore,

Table 8–2. The Noddings-Calamos low-risk convertible bond index

Year	*No. of Bonds*	*No. of Preferreds*	*Total No. of Issues**
1976	10	3	13
1977	28	8	36
1978	27	26	53
1979	27	31	58
1980	28	24	52
1981	24	8	32
1982	40	10	50
1983	52	5	57
1984 (6 mos.)	30	†	30

* Number of convertibles for each year = number in the account at the beginning of the year + new convertibles purchased during the year. The occasional sale and subsequent repurchase of the same security during the year counts as an additional issue.

† Convertible preferreds were dropped from the index beginning in 1984.

a 1.5 percent charge was assigned to each trade (3 percent round trip), to assure a fair performance representation. This expense factor should approximate normal management fees and brokerage commissions. No other market indexes or averages take ongoing expenses into account; that is why it is extremely difficult for traditional money managers to outperform indexes. Even the S&P 500 and DJIA are "managed" to some extent by changing the companies which make up those indexes.

Table 8–2 presents an annual breakdown on the number of issues involved in the index each year, beginning in 1976. Appendix C provides a complete listing of all 252 convertibles employed over the 8.5-year period, including trade dates plus purchase and sale prices.

PERFORMANCE MEASUREMENT

Table 8–3 compares the index's quarterly performance calculations to quarterly returns for Standard & Poor's 500 Stock Index, Salomon Brothers High-Grade Corporate Bond Index, and a 50/50 combination of the two: the balanced approach.

Table 8–3. Quarterly returns for the Noddings-Calamos low-risk convertible bond index and appropriate market indexes

Year	*Quarter*	*Common Stocks*	*Corporate Bonds*	*Balanced Approach*	*Low-Risk Convertible Bond Index*
1976	1	+ 15.0%	+ 4.2%	+ 9.6%	+ 18.0%
	2	+ 2.4	+ 0.3	+ 1.4	+ 4.9
	3	+ 1.9	+ 5.6	+ 3.8	+ 5.5
	4	+ 3.1	+ 7.5	+ 5.3	+ 6.1
1977	1	− 7.5	− 2.3	− 4.9	− 1.4
	2	+ 3.2	+ 3.9	+ 3.6	+ 6.2
	3	− 2.8	+ 1.1	− 0.8	− 1.3
	4	− 0.3	− 0.8	− 0.6	+ 1.4
1978	1	− 4.9	0	− 2.4	+ 2.4
	2	+ 8.5	− 1.1	+ 3.7	+ 11.1
	3	+ 8.7	+ 3.1	+ 5.9	+ 8.1
	4	− 5.0	− 2.0	− 3.5	− 9.8

Table 8–3 (*continued*)

Year	*Quarter*	*Common Stocks*	*Corporate Bonds*	*Balanced Approach*	*Low-Risk Convertible Bond Index*
1979	1	+ 7.1	+ 1.6	+ 4.4	+ 9.3
	2	+ 2.7	+ 4.5	+ 3.6	+ 6.8
	3	+ 7.6	− 2.0	+ 2.8	+ 6.0
	4	+ 0.1	− 7.9	− 3.9	− 3.1
1980	1	− 4.1	−13.5	− 8.8	− 6.5
	2	+ 13.5	+25.1	+ 19.3	+ 20.7
	3	+ 11.2	−11.1	0	+ 14.2
	4	+ 9.5	+ 1.2	+ 5.4	+ 0.2
1981	1	+ 1.4	− 1.1	+ 0.2	+ 7.6
	2	− 2.3	− 2.2	− 2.2	+ 4.8
	3	− 10.3	− 9.3	− 9.8	− 9.9
	4	+ 6.9	+12.9	+ 9.9	+ 10.9
1982	1	− 7.3	+ 3.6	− 1.8	− 5.7
	2	− 0.6	+ 2.5	+ 1.0	− 3.4
	3	+ 11.5	+21.4	+ 16.4	+ 11.6
	4	+ 18.2	+11.5	+ 14.8	+ 12.9
1983	1	+ 10.0	+ 3.7	+ 6.8	+ 13.0
	2	+ 11.1	+ 1.3	+ 6.2	+ 12.2
	3	− 0.2	− 0.3	− 0.2	− 1.6
	4	+ 0.4	− 0.1	+ 0.2	− 2.2
1984	1	− 2.4	− 1.4	− 1.9	− 1.4
	2	− 2.6	− 4.6	− 3.3	− 1.5
Cumulative return		+157.4%	+57.4%	+106.7%	+282.3%

Exhibit 8–1 compares the three indexes graphically by adjusting each to a starting value of 100 at the beginning of 1976. The shaded areas of the graph represent advancing markets (as determined by the S&P 500); the nonshaded areas are declining markets. The initial time period, "A," started midway through a two year market advance beginning in

Exhibit 8–1. The Noddings-Calamos low-risk convertible bond index versus appropriate market indexes

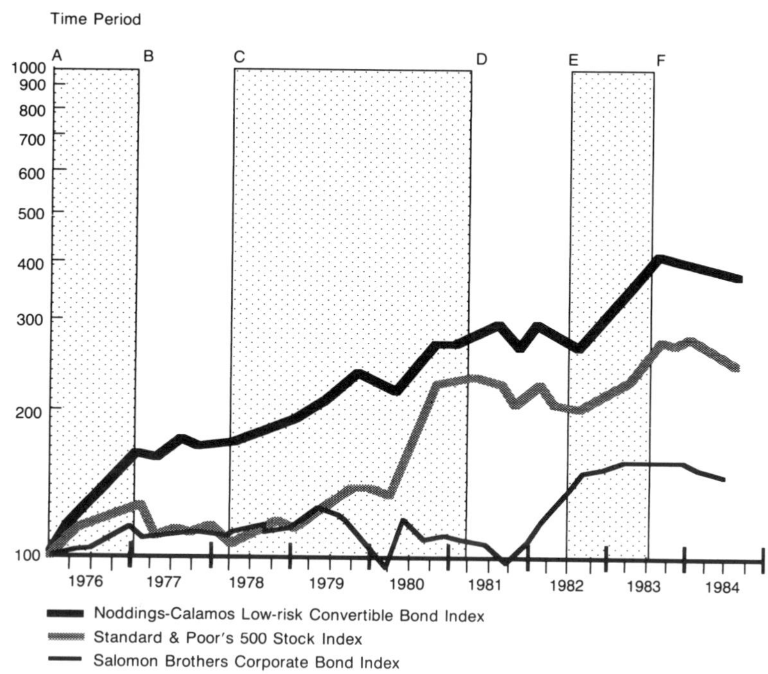

1975. Covering nearly three full market cycles, the 8.5-year period should permit a reasonable comparison of low-risk convertible securities with their stock and bond counterparts.

Table 8–4 compares the indexes based on annual rates of return. Table 8–5 presents a comparison based on market cycles. The returns for the 8.5-year period were:

	Cumulative Returns	*Annualized Returns*
Common stocks	+157%	+11.7%
Corporate bonds	+ 57%	+ 5.5%
Balanced approach	+106%	+ 8.9%
Low-risk convertibles	+282%	+17.0%

Table 8–4. The Noddings-Calamos low-risk convertible bond index compared with appropriate market indexes—annual performance data

	*Common Stocks**	*Corporate Bonds†*	*Balanced Approach‡*	*Low-Risk Convertible Index*
1976	+ 23.6%	+18.6%	+ 21.4%	+ 38.6%
1977	− 7.2	+ 1.7	− 2.9	+ 4.8
1978	+ 6.6	− 0.1	+ 3.4	+ 10.9
1979	+ 18.4	− 4.2	+ 6.8	+ 19.9
1980	+ 32.5	− 2.6	+ 15.1	+ 29.1
1981	− 5.0	− 1.0	− 2.9	+ 12.7
1982	+ 21.6	+43.7	+ 32.5	+ 14.8
1983	+ 22.5	+ 4.7	+ 13.4	+ 22.0
1984 (6 months)	− 5.0	− 5.9	− 5.4	− 2.9
Cumulative return for 8.5 years	+157.4%	+57.4%	+106.7%	+282.3%
Annualized return	+ 11.7%	+ 5.5%	+ 8.9%	+ 17.0%

* Standard & Poor's 500 Stock Index with dividends reinvested.
† Salomon Brothers High Grade Long-Term Corporate Bond Index with interest reinvested.
‡ 50/50 stock-bond combination, rebalanced quarterly.

Table 8–5. The Noddings-Calamos low-risk convertible bond index compared with appropriate market indexes—cycle analysis

Time Period	*Common Stocks*	*Corporate Bonds*	*Balanced Approach*	*Low-Risk Convertible Index*
A. 4 quarters beginning 12–75	+ 23.6%	+18.6%	+ 21.4%	+ 38.6%
B. 5 quarters beginning 12–76	− 11.9	+ 1.7	− 5.3	+ 7.4
C. 12 quarters beginning 3–78	+ 78.2	− 7.8	+ 30.6	+ 80.2
D. 5 quarters beginning 3–81	− 13.7	+ 6.3	− 4.0	− 4.5
E. 4 quarters beginning 6–82	+ 61.3	+42.1	+ 51.7	+ 59.8
F. 4 quarters beginning 6–83	− 4.7	− 6.3	− 5.5	− 6.5
Cumulative return for 8.5 yrs.	+157.4%	+57.4%	+106.7%	+282.3%

PERFORMANCE EVALUATION

In spite of the fact that portfolios making up the low-risk convertible bond index were never broadly diversified, the index tracked the Standard & Poor's surprisingly well (Exhibit 8–1). During the six advancing years (Table 8–4), the convertibles outperformed the S&P 500 three times and underperformed it three times. The key to its overall success was down-year performance; in each case low-risk convertibles did better than common stocks. By preserving capital during declining markets, low-risk convertibles *significantly* outperformed higher-risk common stocks over nearly three full market cycles.

Direct comparisons of the convertible index against corporate bonds or the balanced approach is a more difficult task. Since straight corporate bonds performed so poorly (except for 1976 and 1982), I cannot conclude that low-risk convertibles can always be expected to outperform the balanced approach to the extent experienced thus far (+17.0 percent versus +8.9 percent annualized returns). In fact, I would not anticipate such a large divergence in the future. Convertible bonds should outperform the balanced approach (Appendix B) by *more than normal expectations* during periods of rising stock prices combined with falling bond prices. This was our experience over the six-year period prior to the 1982 bond market surge, and again in 1983. Perhaps convertibles should be looked at simply as a low-risk alternative to the stock market and not attempt to measure them against stocks and bonds in combination with each other.

CONSTRUCTIVE CRITICISM WELCOME

Performance evaluation of any investment strategy over *short* periods of time hinders the ability to understand and appreciate true, *long-term* merits or drawbacks. This is especially true for strategies involving hybrid securities. When it comes to convertible bonds, most investors seem to fall into three distinctly different camps. One recognizes their inherent advantages. The other two ignore them, one through lack of knowledge and the other in the belief that all securities are efficiently priced. We are in frequent contact with numerous professionals who understand, appreciate, and use convertibles; however, we seldom hear from those who feel otherwise.

One recent exception is a financial reporter who questioned the integrity of our two convertible indexes in a hastily written article on performance evaluation (*Forbes,* June 18, 1984). His major concern seemed to be that these high-return indexes are not based on the securities *currently* held by our largest account (see Account selection, page 86). Although given its performance data, he failed to disclose that this account has actually *outperformed* the indexes.

Indexes are not infallible! Any index has its flaws. Let's examine the highly touted Dow Jones Industrial Average. Not only is the DJIA poorly diversified by number of securities and industry classifications, but it strongly favors high-priced stocks. A given percentage move in a $100 stock such as IBM has ten times the impact, on the average, as the same percentage move for a $10 stock such as International Harvester. As poorly performing stocks drop in price, they have less and less influence, and may ultimately be replaced by higher-priced issues (trading below $10, Chrysler was recently replaced by IBM). As successful stocks rise in price their influence becomes greater—that is, until they split. If IBM, for instance, split two for one it would, all at once, impact the Dow average by only half what it did the day before. (Its influence on the S&P 500 would remain the same.) It seems the Dow is destined to be dominated by mediocre performers. This is probably why it has underperformed broader indexes over the years and why professional investors do not consider it a good yardstick for performance evaluation.

Our convertible indexes give equal weight to each security. I believe this, in conjunction with the other factors detailed in the discussion on construction parameters, helps to provide a fair representation of the convertible opportunities available. The indexes' main weakness is diversification; we will probably never see the number of *attractive* issues needed to provide perfect diversification. Thus, we can continue to expect abnormal divergences, both favorable and unfavorable, from broader market standards such as the S&P 500.

Noddings, Calamos & Associates' policy has always been to present our investment strategies in a carefully thought out, forthright, and well documented manner through our books, articles, and investment workshops. We will continue to share our market experiences via indexes and other representations (as in this book), and will always welcome both suggestions for improvement and constructive criticism.

NOTES FOR CHAPTER 8

1. Thomas C. Noddings, *The Investor's Guide to Convertible Bonds,* Dow Jones-Irwin, 1982.

CHAPTER 9

A Superior Alternative to Common Stocks

Chapters 7 and 8 urged the use of undervalued low-risk convertible bonds as superior alternatives to traditional high-quality stocks and straight bonds. This chapter moves up a notch on the convertible strategies line and introduces *aggressive* convertibles as an unparalleled alternative to the stock market itself.

AGGRESSIVE CONVERTIBLES VERSUS THE CAPITAL MARKET LINE

By my definition, an *aggressive* convertible bond can be one of two radically different securities. It can be either a high-quality issue trading well above par or, more typically, a convertible bond trading near par whose common stock is considered to be speculative.

First, let's take a quick look at the first type. Trading high on its price curve (e.g., 120 to 140), the convertible's total return can be expected to match the future profit potential of its underlying common stock at not much more than half its downside risk. These aggressive, high-quality issues fall in the lower end of the range of Exhibit 9–1 at a risk level below the S&P 500. A diversified portfolio of such attractive securities should be viewed as a *low-risk* alternative to a high-quality common stock portfolio; it can be compared directly with the S&P 500, since interest rate changes and resulting bond market price swings have little impact on convertible bonds in the 120 to 140 price range (Appendix B). Yet a word of caution is in order. Since most companies intend to call their

Exhibit 9–1. Undervalued aggressive convertible bonds compared to the capital market line

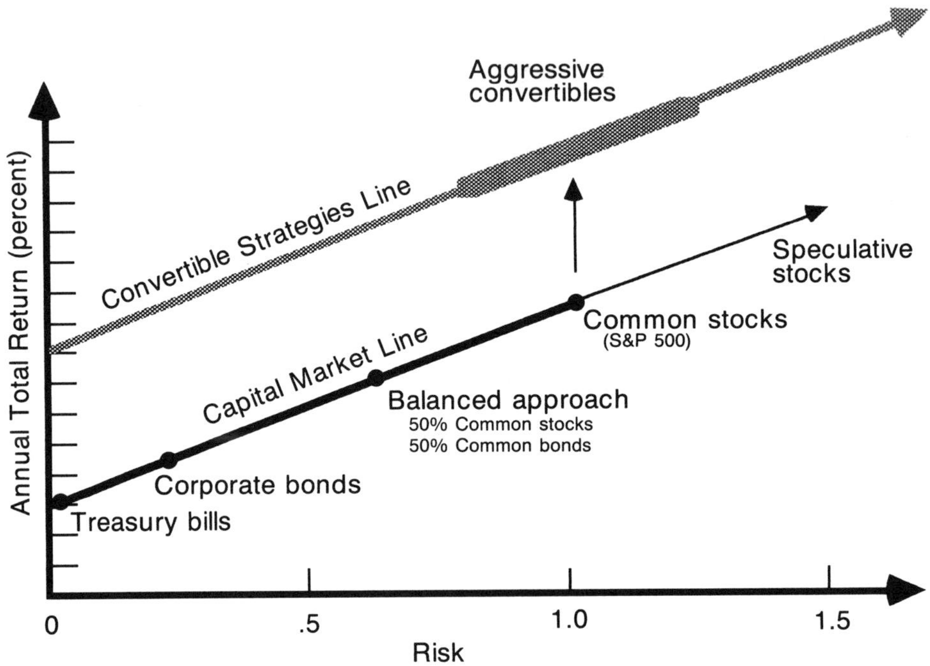

convertibles at the earliest opportunity, make sure that any purchase candidate has call protection through its next semi-annual interest payment date. The practice of calling in higher-priced convertibles limits the number of opportunities available. Therefore, these aggressive, high-quality issues should probably be looked at as a small adjunct to your portfolio's core holdings of low-risk convertibles trading near par.

The second type of aggressive convertible will normally be as frequently available as the low-risk issues of Chapters 7 and 8. Their lower-quality stocks will usually be ranked *below* B+ by Standard & Poor's. Table 9–1 presents a 10-issue sample portfolio available in June 1984.

Excluding, for a moment, its yield advantage, the sample convertible bond portfolio (Table 9–1) offered more than two-thirds the upside potential (+69 percent versus +100 percent) at less than half the risk (−22

Table 9–1. Undervalued aggressive convertible bonds available in June 1984

Company Name	Bond Description	Bond Price	Current Yield	Leverage* −50 Percent	Leverage* +100 Percent	Volatility†
Andersen Group	10.50–02	92	11.4%	−18%	+53%	155
Beefsteak Charlies	13.00–97	83	15.7	−18	+60	175
Computer Consoles	7.75–98	99	7.8	−26	+68	150
Crime Control	10.00–97	95	10.5	−19	+53	165
Data-Design Labs	12.25–00	117	10.5	−24	+87	130
Mobile Communications	12.00–02	122	9.8	−27	+91	175
Pan American	15.00–98	114	13.2	−16	+67	140
Prairie Producing	9.25–03	114	8.1	−29	+86	150
Recognition Equipment	11.00–06	97	11.3	−18	+50	175
Telepictures	10.00–02	108	9.3	−25	+74	155
Averages (10 positions)			10.8%	−22%	+69%	155

* The estimated percent change for the convertible for changes in the price of the underlying stock of −50 or +100 percent.

† Volatility is a measurement of a stock's past price fluctuations compared to the average stock having a 100 volatility.

Source: Noddings, Calamos & Associates' research.

percent versus −50 percent) of the underlying common stocks. Since most of the stocks paid little or no dividends, almost all of the convertible portfolio's 10.8 percent current yield will add to its potential, and reduce its risk, in a *total-return* risk-reward comparison.

Institutional investors ignore this particular sector of the convertible securities market by a greater extent than the low-risk sector. Issue sizes are often rather small (below $25 million) making institutional-size purchases and sales extremely difficult. Also, many institutions simply avoid speculative companies. Thus, careful research will frequently uncover unbelievable aftermarket bargains in the secondary market sector.

Broadly diversified portfolios of aggressive, low-quality convertible bonds should be viewed as *high-return* stock market alternatives; they would fall in the mid- to upper area of the range (Exhibit 9–1). Their future price action, however, will often diverge from a high-quality index like the S&P 500. Hence, other indicators such as the volatile American Stock Exchange and National Association of Security Dealers Composite Indexes should be considered when evaluating performance.

PORTFOLIO MANAGEMENT

Managing a portfolio of aggressive convertible bonds uses tools and guidelines similar to those used with low-risk issues (Chapter 7). The major exception is stock beta ratings. Stocks of companies in Table 9–1 are much more volatile than the average, but their price actions often do not track the high-quality sector of the market. Thus, their beta ratings based on the S&P 500 can be misleadingly low. For this reason, I avoid betas and look instead at the stock's volatility ratings (available from *Value Line Convertibles*). Volatility numbers in the sample portfolio (Table 9–1) ranged from 130 to 175, well above the 100 base of average stocks.

THE NODDINGS-CALAMOS AGGRESSIVE CONVERTIBLE BOND INDEX

Another useful portfolio management tool is the Noddings-Calamos aggressive convertible bond index. Like our low-risk index, this indicator documents market opportunities. The difference is that it deals in opportunities at higher levels of risk. It too is based on actual purchases and sales.

Account selection. The same accounts used for the low-risk index were employed in selecting securities for the aggressive index from 1976 through 1982. Beginning in 1983, we chose a different managed portfolio containing a heavier concentration in the aggressive market sector. As a result, we achieved greater diversification—29 positions as of mid-1984. Five different accounts have been involved in the index over the 8.5 years; the last choice has been in use for 1.5 years. Owing to its unique design, favoring aggressive convertible bonds, I expect its continued use in the foreseeable future.

Security selection. Until 1984, all aggressive candidates had underlying common stocks ranked below B+ by Standard & Poor's. The index now includes B+ stocks if they are not listed on the New York Stock Exchange. Beginning in early 1983, the selection criteria were modified to include bonds trading in the over-the-counter market and to exclude all convertible preferreds. Like changes made to the S&P 500 and DJIA to maintain their worth as reliable market indicators of high quality stocks,

Table 9–2. The Noddings-Calamos aggressive convertible bond index, positions held on June 30, 1984

Company Name	*Bond Description*	*Bond Price*	*Current Yield*	*Vola-tility*	*S&P Stock Rank*
American Adventure	10.00 –98	112.00	8.9%	175	NR
American Century Corp.	6.75 –91	72.00	9.4	145	NR
American Maize Products	11.75 –00	105.00	11.2	125	B
Anacomp	13.875–02	51.50	12.6*	160	B
Andersen Group	10.50 –02	91.00	11.5	155	B+
Beefsteak Charlies	13.00 –97	83.00	15.7	230	B–
Carl Karcher Enterprises	9.50 –07	125.50	7.6	120	NR
Computer Consoles	7.75 –98	102.50	7.6	150	B
Comserv Corp.	11.00 –02	38.50	0†	165	B+
CPT Corp.	10.00 –01	80.00	12.5	140	B+
Crime Control	10.00 –97	93.00	10.8	165	NR
Crystal Oil	11.375–00	77.00	14.8	155	B–
Data-Design Labs	12.25 –00	118.50	10.4	130	B+
Delmed	10.50 –02	69.00	15.2	125	NR
Graphic Scanning	10.00 –01	64.00	15.6	185	C
Inter-Regional Financial	10.00 –03	63.50	15.8	125	B
Koger Properties	9.25 –03	85.00	10.9	160	B
Lear Petroleum	9.00 –03	83.25	10.8	145	B
MGM Grand Hotels	9.50 –00	82.50	11.5	135	NR
Mobile Communications	12.00 –02	114.50	10.5	175	NR
Pan American	15.00 –98	112.50	13.3	140	C
Prairie Producing	9.25 –03	111.00	8.3	150	NR
Pulte Home	8.50 –08	74.00	11.5	145	B
Recognition Equipment	11.00 –06	93.50	11.8	175	C
Southwest Forest Ind.	10.00 –03	118.50	8.4	135	C
Telepictures	10.00 –02	107.00	9.4	155	NR
US Air Group	9.25 –07	111.50	8.3	130	B
Walker Communications	11.00 –99	101.00	10.9	165	NR
Western Air Lines	14.00 –98	87.00	16.1	150	C
Averages (29 positions)			11.1%	152	

* Based on an exchange offer package involving new convertible bonds and convertible preferred stock made 6–29–84 to holders of the 13.875s of 2002.

† Company announced on 7–3–84 that it did not make its interest payment due 7–1–84. It is attempting to arrange a bank credit line in time to pay the interest within the 30-day grace period.

our aggressive convertible bond index is refined, as conditions warrant, to keep it abreast of opportunities available in the secondary convertible market sector. Table 9–2 lists the index's 29 convertible bonds as of June 30, 1984. Of the 29 underlying common stocks, 12 were New York listed, 6 were on the American Exchange, and 11 were OTC traded.

Weighting. All aggressive convertibles are given equal representation as those in the low-risk index.

Minimum position size. A minimum position size is employed as with the low-risk index.

Pricing. Actual purchase and sale prices are used as with the low-risk index.

Management and trading expenses. A 3 percent roundtrip expense factor is also applied to all trades.

An annual breakdown of the issues involved in the index is presented in Table 9–3. Appendix D provides a complete listing of all 175 convertibles over the 8.5 year period, including trade dates and purchase and sale prices.

Table 9–3. The Noddings-Calamos aggressive convertible bond index

Year	*No. of Bonds*	*No. of Preferreds*	*Total No. of Issues**
1976	7	1	8
1977	13	2	15
1978	23	3	26
1979	16	4	20
1980	23	4	27
1981	40	3	43
1982	43	4	47
1983	46	†	46
1984 (6 mos.)	37	†	37

* Number of convertibles for each year = number in the account at the beginning of the year + new convertibles purchased during the year. The occasional sale and subsequent repurchase of the same security during the year counts as an additional issue.

† Convertible preferreds were dropped from the index beginning in 1983.

Table 9–4. Quarterly returns for the Noddings-Calamos aggressive convertible bond index and appropriate stock market indexes

Year	*Quarter*	*S&P 500 Index*	*NASDAQ Composite Index*	*AMEX Index*	*Aggressive Convertible Bond Index*
1976	1	+ 15.0%	+ 11.9%	+ 24.9%	+ 9.7%
	2	+ 2.4	− 0.3	+ 1.0	+ 9.0
	3	+ 1.9	+ 1.0	− 3.2	+ 6.1
	4	+ 3.1	+ 7.3	+ 7.7	+ 4.9
1977	1	− 7.5	− 3.8	+ 1.2	+ 1.5
	2	+ 3.2	+ 5.9	+ 8.2	+ 4.9
	3	− 2.8	+ 1.1	− 1.2	+ 0.5
	4	− 0.3	+ 4.2	+ 7.6	+ 1.9
1978	1	− 4.9	+ 1.1	+ 0.8	+ 10.6
	2	+ 8.5	+ 13.0	+ 12.9	+ 10.4
	3	+ 8.7	+ 10.7	+ 16.0	+ 14.7
	4	− 5.0	− 11.3	− 10.8	− 6.9
1979	1	+ 7.1	+ 11.8	+ 19.4	+ 13.9
	2	+ 2.7	+ 4.8	+ 11.7	+ 8.4
	3	+ 7.6	+ 8.6	+ 2.2	+ 8.5
	4	+ 0.1	+ 0.8	+ 20.4	+ 2.1
1980	1	− 4.1	− 13.3	− 5.7	− 4.2
	2	+ 13.5	+ 20.4	+ 26.0	+ 15.7
	3	+ 11.2	+ 19.0	+ 12.9	+ 11.2
	4	+ 9.5	+ 7.8	+ 5.3	+ 7.2
1981	1	+ 1.4	+ 3.9	+ 3.3	+ 11.8
	2	− 2.3	+ 3.1	+ 3.9	+ 1.5
	3	− 10.3	− 16.9	− 21.8	− 12.1
	4	+ 6.9	+ 8.3	+ 9.5	+ 4.7
1982	1	− 7.3	− 9.9	− 18.9	− 0.3
	2	− 0.6	− 2.5	− 3.6	+ 2.2
	3	+ 11.5	+ 9.5	+ 12.9	+ 8.8
	4	+ 18.2	+ 23.9	+ 20.3	+ 18.0
1983	1	+ 10.0	+ 16.5	+ 14.2	+ 12.3
	2	+ 11.1	+ 17.7	+ 24.6	+ 20.0
	3	− 0.2	− 6.9	− 5.0	− 7.6
	4	+ 0.4	− 6.1	− 3.1	− 1.4
1984	1	− 2.4	− 10.0	− 5.4	+ 1.2
	2	− 2.6	− 4.4	− 5.1	− 7.2
Cumulative return		+157.4%	+196.0%	+379.4%	+438.5%

PERFORMANCE MEASUREMENT

Table 9–4 compares quarterly performance calculations to quarterly returns for Standard & Poor's 500 Stock Index, NASDAQ Index, and the American Stock Exchange Index. Adjusting each index to a starting base of 100 at the beginning of 1976 allows a graphic comparison of the four indexes (Exhibit 9–2).

Table 9–5 compares the same indexes based on annual rates of return; Table 9–6 compares them based on market cycles. The returns for the 8.5 year period were:

	Cumulative Returns	*Annualized Returns*
Standard & Poor's 500	+157%	+11.7%
NASDAQ Composite	+196	+13.6
American Stock Exchange	+379	+20.2
Average of the three indexes	+239	+15.4
Aggressive convertibles	+438	+21.8

PERFORMANCE EVALUATION

Roger Ibbotson's and Rex Sinquefield's *Stocks, Bonds, Bills and Inflation: The Past and the Future* documents how common stocks of smaller companies listed on the New York Stock Exchange have outperformed the S&P 500. Their over-achievement has been profoundly evident since the end of the 1974 bear market, a period dominated by the institutional money managers. A review of the 175 issues used in our aggressive convertible bond index (Appendix D) reveals that many of the stocks underlying the convertibles would probably fit a small-company label, especially since 1983, when over-the-counter issues were added to the index.

Unfortunately, a market index which measures performance of the smaller New York Stock Exchange companies does not exist. They are included in the New York Stock Exchange Index itself, but since the NYSE index is weighted by market value, their influence is heavily overshadowed. Therefore, I turned to the National Association of Security

Exhibit 9–2. The Noddings-Calamos aggressive convertible bond index versus appropriate market indexes

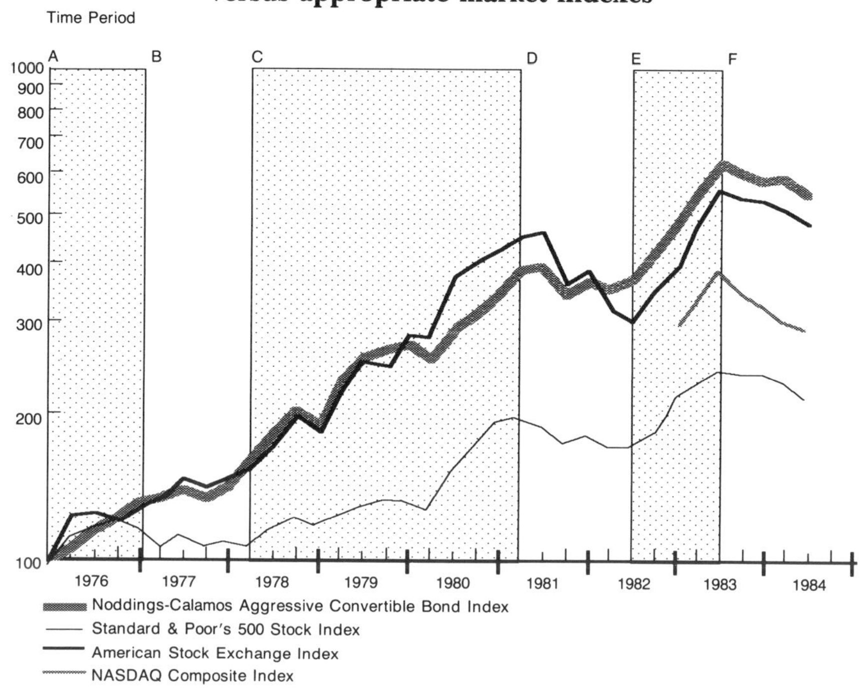

Dealers Composite Index (NASDAQ) for over-the-counter stocks and the American Stock Exchange Index (AMEX) as possible proxies for smaller companies. Perhaps the market environment within which we work when selecting aggressive convertibles might be best approximated by some combination of the S&P 500, the NASDAQ, and the AMEX indexes. (Table 9–5 includes an average of the three).

Exhibit 9–2 clearly shows major divergences between the NASDAQ, the AMEX and the S&P 500 indexes, just as we would be expect. In 1977, for example, the S&P dropped 7.2 percent while the AMEX *gained* 16.4 percent (Table 9–5). Propelled by the energy crisis, the AMEX, having a large number of small energy companies, far outdistanced the S&P 500 through 1980. The five year period from 1976 through 1980 saw the AMEX rise 318 percent, while the S&P 500 rose only 91 percent.

Table 9–5. The Noddings-Calamos aggressive convertible bond index compared with appropriate market indexes—annual performance data

	*S&P 500 Index**	*NASDAQ Index†*	*AMEX Index‡*	*Average§*	*Aggressive Convertibles*
1976	+ 23.6%	+ 20.9%	+ 31.6%	+ 25.4%	+ 33.1%
1977	− 7.2	+ 7.3	+ 16.4	+ 5.5	+ 9.0
1978	+ 6.6	+ 12.2	+ 17.7	+ 12.2	+ 30.4
1979	+ 18.4	+ 28.2	+ 64.1	+ 36.9	+ 36.8
1980	+ 32.5	+ 33.9	+ 41.2	+ 35.9	+ 32.1
1981	− 5.0	− 3.6	− 8.1	− 5.6	+ 4.4
1982	+ 21.6	+ 19.2	+ 6.2	+ 15.7	+ 30.8
1983	+ 22.5	+ 19.9	+ 31.0	+ 24.5	+ 22.8
1984 (6 mos.)	− 5.0	− 14.0	− 10.3	− 9.8	− 6.1
Cumulative return for 8.5 years	+157.4%	+196.0%	+379.4%	+238.7%	+438.5%
Annualized return	+ 11.7%	+ 13.6%	+ 20.2%	+ 15.4%	+ 21.8%

* Standard & Poor's Stock Index with dividends reinvested.
† The National Association of Security Dealer's Composite Index.
‡ The American Stock Exchange Index.
§ Average of the S&P 500, NASDAQ, and AMEX indexes, rebalanced annually.

Table 9–6. The Noddings-Calamos aggressive convertible bond index compared with appropriate market indexes—cycle analysis

Time Period	*S&P 500 Index*	*NASDAQ Index*	*AMEX Index*	*Aggressive Convertible Index*
A. 4 quarters beginning 12–75	+ 23.6%	+ 20.9%	+ 31.6%	+ 33.1%
B. 5 quarters beginning 12–76	− 11.9	+ 8.5	+ 17.4	+ 20.6
C. 12 quarters beginning 3–78	+ 78.2	+ 97.9	+179.6	+138.1
D. 5 quarters beginning 3–81	− 13.7	− 18.5	− 30.5	− 4.8
E. 4 quarters beginning 6–82	+ 61.3	+ 86.0	+ 93.2	+ 57.7
F. 4 quarters beginning 6–83	− 4.7	− 24.8	− 17.4	− 14.4
Cumulative return for 8.5 years	+157.4%	+196.0%	+379.4%	+438.5%

Since 1980, however, the high-quality S&P 500 actually did much better than the AMEX, +35 percent versus only +15 percent.

Aggressive convertibles turned in a surprisingly more consistent performance than the S&P or the speculative NASDAQ and AMEX indexes. The convertible bond index rose in value when any of the three stock market indexes advanced. During the latest 12 months, to mid-1984, its value plummeted along with the NASDAQ and the AMEX; all speculative stocks declined during this 12 month period, not just the AMEX's small energy companies. Overall, aggressive convertibles outperformed all three stock market indexes for the 8.5-year period. They are certainly not stodgy investments.

A review of the securities making up the index as it stood in mid-1984 (Table 9–2) shows a large number of bonds that would qualify as deep discounts (Chapter 6). Thirteen of the 29 issues, for instance, were trading at 85 or below. In the past, I was quicker to replace convertibles trading well below par with higher-priced issues to maintain upside potential. However, since the studies referred to in Chapter 6 indicated high potential for deep discounts, and since many of the issues currently held are on more speculative AMEX and OTC companies, my intention is to hold most of these low-priced convertibles for the next market recovery. The two lowest priced bonds in the index deserve special comment.

One, the Anacomp 13.875s of 2002 (51½), illustrates a creative response by a troubled company to help ward off bankruptcy. Having declined from well above par to the low 30s in the spring of 1984, the convertible bond began a gradual recovery to the 50 level as investors hoped the company would announce an exchange offer. The anticipated offer came on June 29, 1984, and involved an exchange for a package of two new securities. Each of the 13.875s become $500 worth of a new 10 percent convertible bond plus 20 shares of a new $.75 convertible preferred. In effect, the package provides less income ($65.00 versus $137.85 per $1,000 bond) but substantially more shares of common stock upon future conversion (205 versus 57.14 shares). At a $2.50 stock price at the time, the conversion value was increased from $143 up to $512. Assuming all bonds were tendered, the company would save about $3.5 million in interest payments due July 15, plus $3.7 million annually. In addition, the company would reduce its balance sheet liabilities by $25 million. The tradeoff would be a large increase in potential future stock dilution, as the new package converts into 10.25 million shares compared to 2.86 million for the original bond. Closing at 51½ on June 30, 1984, the bonds were at their new conversion value. Perhaps Anacomp was offering an unusual opportunity much like the deep-discount Pan American bonds of Chapter 6.

The lowest-priced issue in the index, the Comserv 11.00s of 2002 (38½), illustrates another kind of problem—one facing portfolio managers who employ fundamental analysis. Comserv's convertible bond was placed in the low-risk category when originally purchased in 1983, since the OTC traded common stock was ranked B+ by Standard & Poor's. (It was switched to the aggressive index at the end of the year in line with our selection criteria improvements, requiring NYSE listing, for low-risk convertibles.) As a result of serious losses, the common plummeted from its 1983 high of $18 to under $2 in June 1984. However, Standard & Poor's had yet to reduce the B+ ranking. On July 3, the company advised that it was unable to make its bond interest payment due 7–1–84 but again, Standard & Poor's retained the B+ ranking. Undoubtedly, Standard & Poor's will eventually get around to lowering Comserv's quality ranking. It would be helpful, however, if the service would more closely monitor stocks *it has chosen* to evaluate.

It is extremely difficult, if not impossible, to obtain meaningful fundamental analysis on companies having aggressive convertibles. As with the deep discount convertible bonds of Chapter 6, the proper approach, I believe, is careful selection based on mathematical relationships, and broad portfolio diversification.

CHAPTER 10

Warrants: A Superior Alternative to Speculative Common Stocks

Aggressive convertible bonds are by no means the only non-institutional type securities with high potential for profit. Investors can beat aggressive convertibles if they are willing to accept higher levels of risk. I am talking about *warrants.*

Warrants may be the most esoteric and potentially the most profitable securities available in the financial markets. Frequently issued as "sweeteners" or "equity kickers" with nonconvertible debt instruments such as MCI Communications' billion dollar financing in 1983, initial warrant purchases are usually made by institutional money managers. Later the warrants, trading separately in the aftermarket, tend to become "playthings" for speculators seeking fast action via high leverage. Since speculators often disregard basic security values, warrants may become *grossly* underpriced or overpriced relative to a fair-value standard. *Undervalued* warrants enable experienced investors to gain a significant edge over conventional stock buyers.

A warrant may generally be defined as "a security issued by a company which represents a long-term option to purchase common stock from the company on specified terms." Often referred to as common stock purchase warrants, their terms are sometimes complex, thus providing unusual opportunities for the informed investor and disappointment for others.

Investors experienced with listed put and call options may view warrants as long-term calls, created by the company instead of by option writers. Most new-issue warrants have a 3–5 year life, although a few are longer term. Because of their relatively long life, warrants are much less risky than listed call options, which have only a few months until expiration.

WARRANTS VERSUS THE CAPITAL MARKET LINE

Exhibit 10–1 graphically shows where *undervalued warrants,* with a life of at least 3 years, fall on the convertible strategies line. These carefully

Exhibit 10–1. Undervalued warrants compared to the capital market line

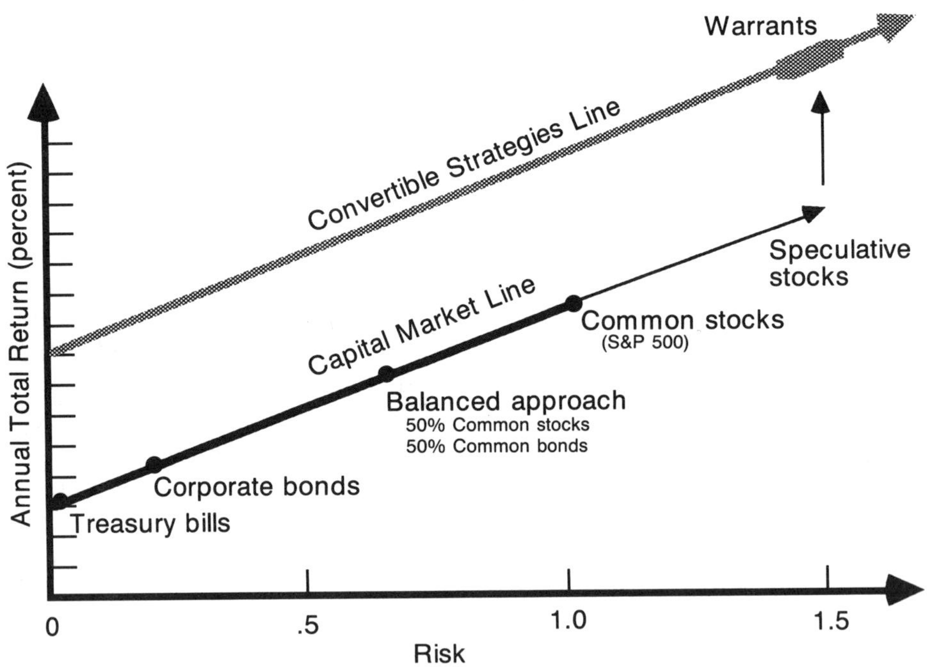

selected securities are a higher-return alternative to speculative common stocks.

Since this book emphasizes strategies for the conservative investor, warrants by themselves would probably be considered too aggressive for most portfolios. However, in a moment I will show how they may be combined with other, lower-risk instruments for low-risk/high-performance investing. First, let's examine a recently issued warrant by the Del E. Webb Corporation to illustrate the high-leverage characteristics of typical new warrant issues brought to the market recently.

THE DEL E. WEBB WARRANT

In April 1984, the Del E. Webb Corp., a diversified company engaged in leisure, real estate, and construction operations, issued $25 million worth of *units.* Each unit consisted of $1,000 principal amount of an 11.5 percent subordinated note due April 15, 1988 and 20 common stock purchase warrants. The units were priced at $955 each, an original issue discount from par.

Although the notes and warrants were not transferable separately prior to June 15, 1984, separate trading markets were immediately available on a when transferable basis. The notes were priced at $895 to yield 14.5 percent to maturity; the warrants were priced at $3.00 each. Del E. Webb's common stock was trading at $16.50 at the time. Were the warrants an attractive purchase candidate or were they a "crap shoot"? Let's evaluate their features and then prepare a risk-reward analysis to look at them as an alternative to purchasing Del E. Webb common.

Exercise terms. Each warrant entitles the holder to purchase one share of the company's common stock for $26.00 (the exercise price), payable at the warrant holder's option in cash, or by surrender of the 11.5s of 1988 notes at 100 percent of their principal amount ($1,000). The $26.00 exercise price is subject to routine adjustment for future events. A two-for-one stock split, for example, would cause a change of the warrant's exercise terms: two shares for $26.00.

Expiration date. The warrants expire on April 15, 1988, four years from the date of issuance (as do the notes). All warrants must be exercised to obtain their conversion value if the stock is trading above $26.00 upon expiration. If they are not exercised, warrant holders will automatically receive one share of common stock for each 100 warrants. This token exchange, valued at $.20 per warrant if, for instance, the common is at $20.00, is necessary under current tax law. It allows the company to avoid the potential tax liability of reporting the original proceeds assigned to the warrant sale as taxable income to the company.

THE WARRANT PRICE CURVE

In my book, *The Dow Jones-Irwin Guide to Convertible Securities* (Dow Jones-Irwin, 1973), I introduced a standardized method for evaluating long-term warrants (three years or more to expiration) against a theoretical normal value. Exhibit 10–2 repeats the normal value curves from the book. We place the Del E. Webb warrant on Exhibit 10–2 through these calculations:

$$S/E = \frac{\text{Stock price}}{\text{Exercise price}} = \frac{\$16.50}{\$26.00} = 0.635$$

$$W/E = \frac{\text{Warrant price}}{\text{Exercise price}} = \frac{\$\ 3.00}{\$26.00} = 0.115$$

From Exhibit 10–2 it would appear that the warrant was quite undervalued and that we should proceed to the risk-reward analysis. However, in recent years, warrant issues have frequently contained a new "wrinkle"—companies can call them just as they can convertible bonds. Del E. Webb can call its warrants at $5.00 each (cash paid by the company) after May 1, 1987, if the common stock is trading above $39.00 (150 percent of the $26.00 exercise price). Since, at a stock price of $39.00, the warrant's conversion value is $13.00 ($39.00 − $26.00), a call would force warrant holders to exercise them prior to their April 15, 1988 expiration date. As with convertible bonds, a pending call will force the warrant toward its conversion value line more quickly than if it had call protection.

Exhibit 10–2. Traditional price curves for long-term warrants (*The Dow Jones-Irwin Guide to Convertible Securities,* page 23)

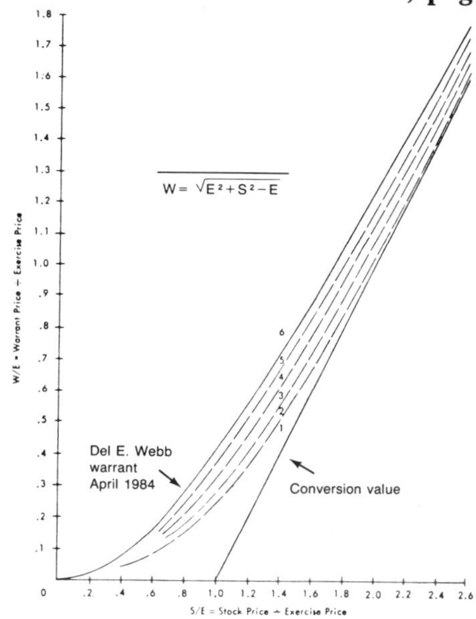

Band 5 = 0-2 percent yield
4 = 2-4 percent
3 = 4-6 percent
2 = 6-8 percent
1 = above 8%

Note: Area 6 represents all warrants above band 5.

Exhibit 10–3 presents a warrant price curve which takes the terms of the call provision into account. The estimated price curve (the solid line) forecasts warrant prices for any stock price 12 months hence; the curve provides prices necessary for preparing a risk-reward analysis.

If the graph of Exhibit 10–3 looks familiar, it should. In essence, it is similar to that portion of a convertible bond graph above the bond's investment value. Convertible bonds are, in reality, a "unit" consisting of a "straight bond" plus a long-term *latent* warrant. When a convertible bond is judged to be undervalued, it is the latent warrant portion of the "unit" that is undervalued. But to take advantage of an attractive convertible, a large portion of one's funds must be tied up in the fairly priced "straight debt" portion. With warrants, one's entire investment can be made directly in the undervalued security, if desired. This advantage is illustrated by the following risk-reward analysis comparing Del E. Webb's warrant directly with its common stock.

Exhibit 10–3. The warrant price curve: Del E. Webb Corporation's 4 year warrant, April 1984 (exercise price = $26.00, expiration date = April 15, 1988, current stock price = $16.50, current warrant price = $3.00)

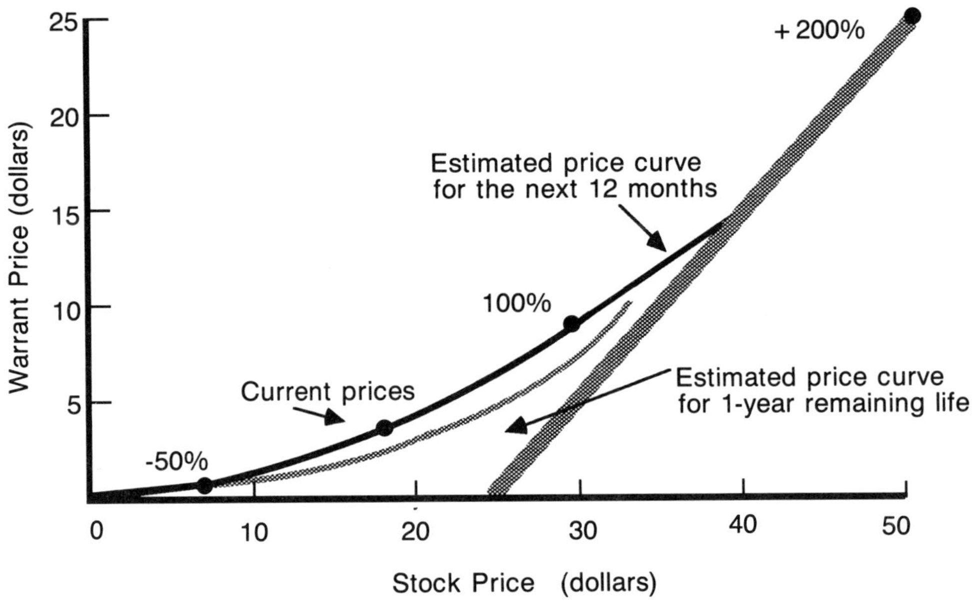

	Stock Price Change in One Year			
	−50 Percent	*0 Percent*	*+100 Percent*	*+200 Percent*
Stock price	8.25	16.50	33.00	49.50
Estimated warrant price	1.00	3.00	10.00	23.50
Stock gain or loss including dividends	−49%	+1%	+101%	+201%
Warrant gain or loss	−67%	0%	+233%	+683%

This risk-reward analysis demonstrates the high-leverage characteristics of many warrants when their underlying common stocks are trading well below the warrant exercise prices (out-of-the-money). These highly-leveraged instruments typically offer two to four times the *near-term* profit potential of their common. The risk-reward tradeoffs are: no dividends, more risk, and price erosion as time passes. (Warrants are a wasting asset and might expire nearly worthless.)

The dashed curve of Exhibit 10–3 estimates warrant prices assuming only one year to maturity. The difference between the two curves indicates expected price deterioration over the next three years. The small differential between the curves is a good indication that the Del E. Webb warrant was undervalued. Warrant purchasers in April 1984 paid but a small *time-value premium* since the expected warrant prices three years hence were not far below current price estimates.

Conservative investors should generally consider only warrants having a remaining life of three years or more and should plan to sell their holdings when the warrant's life drops to one to two years; the final year or two is best left to the speculators. Is there a way for investors who do not wish to own warrants alone, under any circumstances, to take advantage of their undervaluation without exposing their capital to the extra risk? The answer is a resounding yes!

WARRANTS COMBINED WITH CASH

The trick to minimizing risk while still benefiting from undervalued warrants is to combine warrants with cash investments. This places much of one's capital where it can earn a safe, if low, return to offset possible losses on the warrants.

Tables 10–1, 10–2 and 10–3 show risk-reward calculations for varying time frames assuming a 50/50-warrant/cash combination portfolio. The most favorable comparison between the warrant/cash strategy and Del E. Webb's common stock is the one-year workout of Table 10–1. This occurred because the warrant price curve (Exhibit 10–3), being so undervalued, assumed no time-value price deterioration for the first year. At all future stock prices one year hence, the warrant/cash combination outperforms the common stock with the overperformance becoming greater at extreme stock price moves.

Table 10–1. One-year risk-reward analysis: Del E. Webb warrant at $3.00 and cash at 10 percent versus common stock at $16.50

	Stock Price Change in 1 Year			
	−50 Percent	*0 Percent*	*+100 Percent*	*+200 Percent*
Common stock price	$8.25	$16.50	$33.00	$49.50
Estimated warrant price	$1.00	$ 3.00	$10.00	$23.50
Common stock				
Capital gain or loss	−50%	0%	+100%	+200%
Dividends received	+ 1	+ 1	+ 1	+ 1
Total return	−49%	+ 1%	+101%	+201%
50% warrants/50% cash				
Warrants	−67%	0%	+233%	+683%
Cash	+10	+10	+ 10	+ 10
Total return	−28%	+ 5%	+122%	+346%
Warrant/cash advantage	+21%	+ 4%	+ 21%	+145%

Table 10–2. Three-year risk-reward analysis: Del E. Webb warrant at $3.00 and cash at 10 percent versus common stock at $16.50

	Stock Price Change in 3 Years			
	−50 Percent	*0 Percent*	*+100 Percent*	*+200 Percent*
Common stock price	$8.25	$16.50	$33.00	$49.50
Estimated warrant price	$ .50	$ 1.75	$ 9.00	$23.50
Common stock				
Capital gain or loss	−50%	0%	+100%	+200%
Dividends received	+ 4	+ 4	+ 4	+ 4
Total return	−46%	+ 4%	+104%	+204%
50% warrants/50% cash				
Warrants	−83%	−42%	+200%	+683%
Cash	+30	+30	+ 30	+ 30
Total return	−26%	− 6%	+115%	+356%
Warrant/cash advantage	+20%	−10%	+ 11%	+152%

Table 10–3. Four-year risk-reward analysis: Del E. Webb warrant at $3.00 and cash at 10 percent versus common stock at $16.50, 4-year workout

	Stock Price Change in 4 Years			
	−50 Percent	*0 Percent*	*+100 Percent*	*+200 Percent*
Common stock price	$8.25	$16.50	$33.00	$49.50
Estimated warrant price	$ .08	$ .16	$ 7.00	$23.50
Common stock				
Capital gain or loss	−50%	0%	+100%	+200%
Dividends received	+ 5	+ 5	+ 5	+ 5
Total return	−45%	+ 4%	+105%	+205%
50% warrants/50% cash				
Warrants	−97%	−95%	+133%	+683%
Cash	+40	+40	+ 40	+ 40
Total return	−28%	−28%	+ 86%	+362%
Warrant/cash advantage	+17%	−33%	− 19%	+157%

For the three-year holding period shown by Table 10–2, the warrant/cash strategy still does better at most future stock prices; however, it underperforms in a static market.

Table 10–3 illustrates the reason for my earlier statement that warrant positions should be closed out as they come to within one to two years of expiration. As shown, a warrant/cash combination held for the entire four-year period would underperform the common stock over a rather broad price range. As shown by the three risk-reward analysis tables, warrant strategies perform best, relative to common stocks, during volatile markets.

The warrant/cash combination is termed a *synthetic* convertible. An alternative for increasing returns (and risk) would be to construct *fabricated* convertibles by combining the warrants with higher-yielding Del E. Webb 11.5s of 1988 which are usable at par value when exercising the warrants. A third tactic would be to employ two- to three-year U.S. Treasury obligations for greater returns than are normally obtainable from cash, while still achieving the high degree of risk reduction provided by the use of cash.

HISTORICAL PERFORMANCE DATA

My *Dow Jones-Irwin Guide to Convertible Securities* documented a study I conducted on undervalued warrants covering the six years from 1967 through 1972. Table 10–4 and Exhibit 10–4 present the study's results published in the book. Performance calculations for the 22 warrants evaluated over the six year period, compared to their underlying common stocks, are shown in Table 10–4. Also included in the table is a 50/50 warrant/cash combination.

Exhibit 10–4 graphs the 50 percent warrant/50 percent cash combination along with underlying stock performance and the Value Line Stock Index. Note from the exhibit how the warrant/cash strategy kept pace with stocks during the 1967–68 bull market and significantly reduced losses during the ensuing bear market. The warrant/cash combination

Table 10–4. Warrant performance data, a six-year study

	6-Month Profit or Loss		
Six-Month Period	*Common Stock*	*Warrants*	*Warrants and Cash*
January–June 1967	+57.8%	+142.2%	+72.6%
July–December 1967	+25.6	+ 49.7	+26.4
January–June 1968	+89.6	+158.0	+80.5
July–December 1968	+11.8	+ 18.6	+10.8
January–June 1969	−41.8	− 53.2	−25.1
July–December 1969	−25.5	− 29.7	−13.4
January–June 1970	−39.4	− 44.5	−20.8
July–December 1970	+30.1	+ 48.8	+25.9
January–June 1971	+26.6	+ 58.0	+30.5
July–December 1971	+ 1.4	− 3.6	− 0.3
January–June 1972	+ 3.0	+ 5.4	+ 4.2
July–December 1972	− 5.7	− 20.7	− 8.8
Cumulative returns for six years	+ 79%	+ 284%	+ 249%

Source: *The Dow Jones-Irwin Guide to Convertible Securities,* 1973, pages 70–78.

Exhibit 10–4. An early study on warrant performance—1966–'72

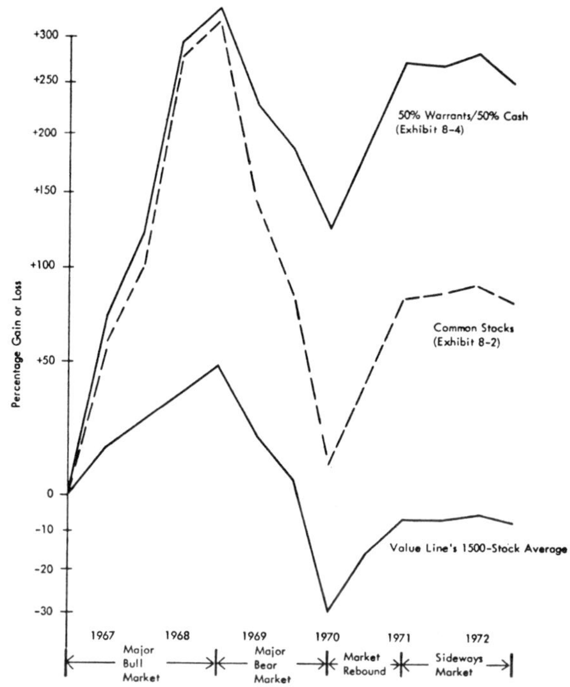

underperformed the underlying common stocks during the static market of the last 1.5 years, as would be expected.

A relative advantage is to be expected when employing *undervalued* securities, but the magnitude of the advantage was surprising—a six year return of 249 percent for the lower-risk warrant/cash strategy versus only 79 percent for their underlying common stocks. The large difference is probably attributable to the unusually high price volatility experienced by those stocks in the study (much higher than the Value Line Stock Index, for instance).

Following the study's completion, the number of long-term warrant opportunities fell drastically as earlier warrants expired and new ones were infrequently issued. However, in recent years warrants have regained their popularity; their universe is now larger than when the study was conducted.

A SAMPLE WARRANT PORTFOLIO

In July 1984, there were about 350 warrants available. Of these, 90 issues were considered to be actively traded and were followed by *Value Line Convertibles.* A list of the companies is included in Appendix F.

Table 10–5 presents a sample portfolio of 10 long-term warrant issues (three or more years of remaining life) having attractive risk-reward characteristics. While these undervalued warrants may have been considered for individual purchase, or combined with money market or debt instruments for risk reduction, they could also have been looked at as a convenient means for adjusting the overall risk-reward posture of one's total portfolio. In July 1984, for instance, we were in the thirteenth month of a broad-based market decline that began in June 1983. Investors holding convertible securities during that market slide undoubtedly saw many issues go to discounts from par value, some probably to deep discounts. Unless those discounted convertible bonds were sold and replaced with convertibles trading near par, the ultra-low-risk portfolios would probably trail well behind common stocks in the next market rise. An alternative would have been the addition of warrants to increase the portfolios' volatility and hence, their performance during the inevitable advance.

Most uninformed investors believe that warrants are issued only by secondary companies. While warrants on speculative stocks usually offer the best risk-reward tradeoffs, even American Telephone & Telegraph, among other blue chips, has employed warrants over the years, a 31 million share AT&T warrant issue expired in 1975. When American Telephone & Telegraph was restructured in 1983, a new AT&T "warrant" emerged on the scene. Called a SCORE component, this unique security was developed by Americus Shareowner Service Corp.

THE AMERICUS TRUST FOR AT&T COMMON SHARES

A prospectus dated October 25, 1983, announced one of the most unusual investment concepts ever introduced by the financial community—the Americus Trust for AT&T common shares. In return for each share of predivestiture AT&T common stock placed in the trust, investors received a *Unit.* The Unit consisted of one *PRIME* component and one *SCORE*

Table 10–5. Undervalued long-term warrants available in July 1984

			*Leverage**		
Company	*Stock Price*	*Warrant Price*	*−50 Percent*	*+100 Percent*	*+200 Percent*
Angeles Corp.	$13.25	$2.38	−66%	+225%	+689%
Beker Industries	6.38	1.75	−60	+177	+431
Collins Foods	18.50	4.00	−67	+235	+606
MCI Communications	8.00	1.44	−60	+179	+438
Nortek	14.25	3.88	−74	+290	+658
Penril	13.25	3.50	−61	+257	+636
Pier 1 Imports	17.25	4.25	−67	+233	+600
Safeguard Scientifics	7.50	2.00	−64	+215	+545
Tyler Corp.	24.50	3.75	−82	+355	+953
Webb, Del E.	17.50	3.62	−68	+243	+631
Averages (10 positions)			−67%	+241%	+619%

* The estimated percent change for the warrant for changes in the price of the underlying stock of −50, +100 or +200 percent over the next 12 months.
Source: Noddings, Calamos & Associates' research.

component; they can be separated from each other by the unitholders at any time and the components sold individually.

Up until the October 24, 1988 termination date, the PRIME component receives all cash dividends *plus* any Unit price appreciation up to $75. The SCORE component receives all price appreciation above $75. Both securities are trading on the New York Stock Exchange.

The SCORE component is, in reality, a *warrant* (or long-term call option) on a package of low-volatility securities having a $75 exercise price and a 10–24–88 expiration date. In July 1984, the Unit was trading at $64.50, the PRIME at $58.00, and the SCORE at $6.50. Considering the fact that holders of the PRIME component were receiving a 9.2 percent current yield plus possible future dividend increases and price appreciation up to $75, the SCORE purchasers at $6.50 were obviously very bullish on Ma Bell and the seven Bell Regional companies. To earn, say, 300 percent on their money over four-plus years (in my judgment a minimum objective when holding a warrant having a high probability of expiring worthless), the Unit must enjoy a 57 percent gain to $101. (The SCORE would be worth $101 − $75 = $26, a 300 percent increase.)

This equates to a total Unit return of about 100 percent when adding back the dividends. Although this event is not impossible, I believed it to be highly unlikely for a package of low-volatility utility stocks. Which security would you have preferred, the PRIME or the SCORE?

This chapter concludes our journey along the convertible strategies line from deep-discount, ultra-low-risk convertible bonds to highly-leveraged warrants. My warrant discussion, intentionally brief, has probably left you, the reader, with a number of questions. Unfortunately, warrants require an entire book to explain all their ramifications. I would normally include information sources for your further study; however, the best books on the subject were written years ago and do not reflect the unusual risks and opportunities of today's new warrant issues. We can hope that someone will prepare a definitive new book on the subject in the near future.

As I promised earlier, you have learned how the convertible securities market offers high-performance alternatives to conventional strategies involving stocks, bonds, or money market instruments. How do you proceed from here? The next chapter introduces professional money managers who employ these strategies. The final chapter presents some very personal thoughts on creating wealth, whether you hire professional management or decide to do it yourself.

CHAPTER 11

Convertible Funds: Professional Money Management at Bargain Prices

All investors face an important, basic question: Does it make more sense to handle their own portfolio, or to engage professional money managers? To a large extent, the answer will depend on the strategies employed. Those who own portfolios of high quality common stocks or long-term bonds and do not plan to sell them, for example, do not require professional management. Those who wish to pursue a sophisticated strategy or a number of different strategies, probably need assistance. Our nation's financial markets have become such diverse and complex beasts that no individual investor, working at it part-time, can possibly be an expert on all available investments. The professional money manager, especially if his is a sophisticated niche, has a substantial edge over today's nonprofessional investor when it comes to competing for maximum return.

As a general rule, I believe, most investors would fare much better if they retained professional help. If they do the job themselves, they almost invariably profit less, and in some cases they may even lose their wealth entirely. The main drawback to hiring professionals is the expense, usually set as a percentage of one's assets under management. That drawback, however, can be eliminated entirely. A skilled professional will not only earn his fees through better performance, but can save on brokerage commissions and related portfolio-management expenses.

Despite the expense, even our nation's largest pension funds typically hire outside managers instead of maintaining professional, in-house money-management staffs. One major fund, for example, employs about thirty outside managers, each having a specific area of expertise ranging from ultra-conservative fixed income to highly aggressive venture capital investing. The company's in-house staff focuses on identifying successful strategies, searches out the top managers who can best implement the strategies, and monitors performance against appropriate market standards. These responsibilities alone require an extremely high level of knowledge and experience; this company correctly believes that *implementation* of the chosen strategies is best left to specialists in their respective fields.

Most large money management firms will not handle separate accounts whose assets are less than $1 million, but investors whose funds exceed $250,000 can find *independent* investment advisors to manage their portfolios. "Smaller" investors with less than $250,000 can also find professional help. However, most small investors will neither do the homework necessary to evaluate market strategies nor seek out competent professionals best able to execute whatever strategies they choose. Most prefer to rely on simplistic (and often costly) advice "freely" rendered by their friends, accountants, doctors, bankers, attorneys, or stockbrokers. While acquaintances or business associates may be highly skilled in their own professions, they usually fail miserably when it comes to money management (just as most money managers would fail if asked to render legal or medical advice). To prove this to yourself, ask your most trusted advisors to explain the intricacies of a convertible bond. You will quickly learn whether or not they are truly savvy investors. Since convertible bonds have been around for a long time and are not nearly as complex as some other financial instruments available in today's markets, this *is* a reasonably fair test of your advisors' competence.

The logical answer for most individual investors is mutual funds, particularly a subgroup called *no-load* funds. Here one can select from a large number of highly skilled management companies having different investment styles. By hiring one or more of these professional no-load managers, investors can design their portfolios to meet highly individualistic risk-reward goals.

This chapter does not attempt to tell you what no-load mutual funds are all about. Suffice it to say that "no-load" means no sales commissions when buying or selling the funds' shares. If you are not knowledgeable in this very important aspect of money management, there are many excellent books available on the subject. I recommend:

1. *The Individual Investor's Guide to No-Load Mutual Funds,* Investment Information Services Press, 205 West Wacker Drive, Chicago, Illinois, 60606. This handbook is published annually by the editors of *The Mutual Fund Letter,* an investment advisory service on no-load mutual funds.
2. *The Handbook for No-Load Fund Investors,* The No-Load Fund Investor, Post Office Box 283, Hastings-on-Hudson, N.Y. 10706. This handbook is published annually by the editors of *The No-Load Fund Investor,* a no-load fund advisory service.

In this chapter, I will focus on investment companies working in the market niche highlighted in this book—the *convertible funds.*

CLOSED-END FUNDS

Closed-end funds can, at times, offer attractive risk-reward opportunities. Unlike mutual (open-end) funds, closed-end funds have fixed capitalizations; that is, they do not continually issue new shares. Buyers and sellers of a fund's shares must execute their orders on the exchange where the fund is listed, just as they would in a normal stock transaction. The agreed-upon price may be at a premium or a discount from net asset value. Funds trading at hefty discounts are the most alluring to experienced investors. Note that closed-end funds are usually identified as publicly traded funds in the financial press.

At present, three closed-end funds specialize in convertible securities. They thereby offer smaller investors the opportunity to gain an edge on the markets with broadly diversified portfolios. However, this is true only if the funds' managers select undervalued situations such as those illustrated in this book. Have they done so? Let us look at how they have performed.

Table 11–1 presents annual performance data for the last five years (1979–83) and compares these funds' results with Standard & Poor's 500 Stock Index. As shown, two of the three (American Capital and

Table 11–1. Closed-end funds specializing in convertible securities—5-year performance data

	American Capital Convertible Fund—ACS	*Bancroft Convertible Fund—BCV*	*Castle Convertible Fund—CVF*	*S&P 500 Index*
1979	+ 21.1%	+ 28.2%	+ 15.6%	+ 18.4%
1980	+ 33.7	+ 33.5	+ 15.0	+ 32.5
1981	+ 6.7	− 6.9	+ 14.9	− 5.0
1982	+ 36.1	+ 11.5	+ 41.3	+ 21.6
1983	+ 25.3	+ 18.7	+ 23.8	+ 22.5
Cumulative return	+195%	+111%	+177%	+122%

Source: Lipper Analytical Services, Inc.

Castle) beat the S&P 500 by wide margins over the five year period, while the third (Bancroft) trailed modestly behind the higher-risk stock index. They have been exceptionally good vehicles for investors seeking income and growth through low-risk investing.

In my book, *Advanced Investment Strategies* (Dow Jones-Irwin, 1978) I recommended purchase of these funds at a time when they were selling at discounts of 19 to 23 percent below their net asset values. Since that time, the funds have outpaced both the stock and bond markets, and, as an extra bonus, their discounts have vanished (as of August 10, 1984 they ranged from a 5.3 percent discount to a 16.2 percent *premium*). Investors, including my own IRA contributions in 1975 and 1976 have received double benefits: market appreciation plus elimination of the large discounts. Are these funds still attractive purchase candidates?

I see no reason to expect that the closed-end convertible funds will not continue to perform as well in the future as they have in the past. Therefore, I would continue to recommend their purchase at any price *below net asset value.* However, a word of caution. The next bear market could cause these funds to trade once again at large discounts just as they did a few years back. Thus, only the very long-term investor who can ride through the market's next down move should consider purchasing them at this time. Be aware also that larger than normal spreads between bid and ask prices, plus brokerage commissions, make them more expensive to obtain than most common stocks; carefully placed limit orders should be used when buying or selling. These funds are not cost free.

LOAD MUTUAL FUNDS

Like the closed-end funds, open-end *mutual* funds (load or no-load) offer broad portfolio diversification and professional management; these are very significant benefits. The load (or front-end load) funds gain their name because they are sold by the funds' sales representatives or stockbrokers at net asset value plus a sales commission (the load). Redemptions are cost-free and are also executed at net asset value. Following is a sales commission table taken from a typical fund prospectus.

Size of Investment	*Sales Commission**
Less than $15,000	9.29%
$15,000 but less than $25,000	8.11
$25,000 but less than $50,000	6.67
$50,000 but less than $100,000	4.99
$100,000 but less than $250,000	3.63
$250,000 but less than $500,000	2.83
$500,000 but less than $1,000,000	2.04
$1,000,000 and over	1.01

* As a percentage of net amount invested.

Considering the fact that a fund's net asset value per share is based on the current market value of the securities it holds, the brokerage commissions and price spreads incurred when setting up its portfolio have already been paid. New investors must pay only the load. While the load is quite high for small amounts, it is probably not much more than if investors were to build their own portfolios and thereby incur the *roundtrip* expenses of buying and selling stocks and/or closed-end funds. Large investors can likely move in and out of a fund at a lower roundtrip cost than if they constructed their own portfolios. So, while I have never employed *load* mutual funds, they are not as costly for most investors as many would lead us to believe.

As this chapter is being written in August 1984, there are four mutual funds which specialize in convertibles; all have front-end loads. How do they compare?

Annual performance data from 1979–83 are shown in Table 11–2. Of the four funds, three outperformed the S&P 500. Only one underperformed, further proof that convertible securities do offer substantial advantages.

Do not arbitrarily assume from Table 11–2 that the best performer (American Capital Harbor Fund) had better management expertise than the fourth place finisher (Convertible Yield Securities). As demonstrated throughout this book, convertible strategies can range from very conservative to highly aggressive risk-reward postures. Convertible Yield Securities was the most conservatively managed of the four, while American Capital Harbor Fund was the most aggressively managed. (At the end of 1983, for instance, 38 percent of its portfolio was invested in common stocks—it has not been purely a low-risk convertible fund.) Investors *must* do their homework when matching any money manager's risk-reward stance with their own objectives.

Table 11–3 presents composite returns for the seven funds (closed-end *and* mutual) and compares their performance with the two Noddings-Calamos convertible bond indexes discussed in Chapters 8 and 9. It is interesting to observe that the funds (averaging 151 percent return) did

Table 11–2. Load mutual funds specializing in convertible securities—5-year performance data

	American Capital Harbor Fund	*Convertible Yield Securities*	*Phoenix Convertible Fund*	*Putnam Convertible Fund*	*S&P 500 Index*
1979	+ 23.1%	+ 15.7%	+ 14.6%	+ 18.2%	+ 18.4%
1980	+ 32.7	+ 32.7	+ 26.7	+ 37.3	+ 32.5
1981	− 4.9	+ 4.6	+ 7.0	+ 6.5	− 5.0
1982	+ 39.3	+ 16.3	+ 31.8	+ 25.9	+ 21.6
1983	+ 26.0	+ 11.1	+ 25.5	+ 13.3	+ 22.5
Cumulative return	+173%	+108%	+157%	+146%	+122%

Source: Standard & Poor's 1983 year-end stock guide.

Table 11–3. Convertible funds compared to the Noddings-Calamos convertible bond indexes

	Seven Convertible Funds' Average	*Noddings-Calamos Indexes*	
		Low-Risk Index	*Aggressive Index*
1979	+ 19.5%	+ 19.9%	+ 36.8%
1980	+ 30.2	+ 29.1	+ 32.1
1981	+ 4.0	+ 12.7	+ 4.4
1982	+ 28.9	+ 14.8	+ 30.8
1983	+ 20.5	+ 22.0	+ 22.8
Cumulative return	+151%	+144%	+203%

better than my firm's low-risk index (144 percent) and not as well as our aggressive index (203 percent). This was to be expected, considering the make-up of their portfolios and the somewhat higher expenses in running a fund compared to the charges assigned to the indexes.

AMERICAN CAPITAL HARBOR FUND

The best performer among the mutual funds was the American Capital Harbor Fund, founded in 1956 as the Harbor Fund. This is the oldest of the funds specializing in convertibles. It is also the largest, with assets totaling $185 million at the end of 1983. In its prospectus, the fund illustrates how a $10,000 investment on December 31, 1963, would have grown to $95,066 at the end of 1983, twenty years later. This assumes that all capital gains and dividend distributions were reinvested in additional shares. This 850 percent total appreciation compares with about 400 percent for the S&P 500 and 300 percent for the Dow Jones Industrial Average, assuming reinvestment of dividends for both.

The fund's exceptional long-term performance results reinforce the merits of convertible securities. However, its superior record was not without a few difficult years along the way. At the end of 1968, the initial $10,000 investment would have grown to $23,733, a 137 percent gain in only five years. This compares with 62 percent achieved by the S&P 500. The next six years were trying times for most investment strategies, including those employed by the Harbor Fund. The fund declined 25 percent during 1969–70, rallied by 26 percent during 1971–72, then dropped 17 percent during 1973–74, a net six year loss of 22 percent. The S&P 500's total return was a negative 19 percent.

However, those investors who stuck with the Harbor Fund were more than amply rewarded for their patience. Their share's net asset value increased more than 400 percent during the next nine years through 1983. Yet, I often wonder how many shareholders gave up during the six poor years to search for another manager with a "hotter hand," or left the market completely for the "safe haven" of a money market fund. From the fund's prospectus, it is apparent that many shareholders "threw in the towel." The number of shares outstanding declined steadily from 18,100,000 in 1974 to 9,500,000 in 1980, nearly a 50 percent drop during a period when the fund was turning in spectacular gains. From 1980, the number of shares outstanding has increased modestly to 11,300,000, but this figure probably represents additional redemptions, offset by dividend reinvestments. Who said money management is an easy job?

NO-LOAD MUTUAL FUNDS

For many years, the very existence of no-load mutual funds was unknown except to a relatively few knowledgeable investors. The recent explosive growth of the no-load money market fund industry helped make others aware that professional money management services are available without sales charges. In addition, investors today are far more sophisticated than in the past. Look, for example, at the American Association of Individual Investors' membership growth to nearly 100,000 in just a few years.[1] The AAII, a not-for-profit organization, serves sophisticated investors through its monthly journal, investment seminars, and local chapter meetings. It has been a strong proponent of no-load funds as the best way to obtain portfolio diversification, plus professional money management, at reasonable cost.

Financial planners who operate on a fee-only basis are also strong advocates of no-load mutuals.[2] These *fee-only* professionals, skilled in financial matters of all kinds, are a much better source for unbiased advice than most insurance agents, stockbrokers, bankers, attorneys, or accountants. However, not all the other professionals are uninformed. I know sincere stockbrokers, for instance, who recommend no-loads to their smaller clients.

Having such prominent support by the above groups and others, the no-load fund industry (excluding money market funds) has grown rapidly in recent years. It has reached a size comparable to that of the traditionally dominant load funds. I expect no-loads to be far larger than load mutuals in the not too distant future.

Until recently, the convertible strategies you have learned about in this book were not available to no-load fund buyers. Since no-loads must *sell themselves,* management companies have been unwilling to take the chance with a no-load convertible fund; investors will simply not buy something they don't understand (such as convertibles) unless it is recommended by a "trusted advisor," usually one who is earning a commission. All *convertible funds* to date, closed-end and load, have been sold by stockbrokers earning hefty commissions.

My firm, Noddings-Calamos Asset Management, decided to fill this void and bring out two distinctly different no-load convertible funds. One, our Convertible Income Fund, is structured for income, with capital appreciation as a secondary objective. The other, our Convertible Growth Fund, is designed for capital growth, with income secondary. As you might suspect from reading this book, the income fund will concentrate on discounted and low-risk convertibles; the growth fund will use aggressive convertibles and warrants. Between the two funds, we plan to take advantage of *all* undervalued convertible and warrant strategies, as illustrated by the convertible strategies line throughout this book.

For your convenience, Table 11–4 lists the addresses and phone numbers for all funds discussed in this chapter. You may call or write them for a no-obligation copy of their prospectus (load and no-load mutual funds) or annual report (closed-end funds). I urge you to investigate this market niche. In my opinion, it is the *only* area of the markets offering professional money management at *bargain prices!*

Table 11–4. Addresses for convertible funds

CLOSED-END FUNDS

American Capital Convertible Securities, Inc.
2777 Allen Parkway, Houston, Texas 77019
(713) 522–1111

Bancroft Convertible Fund, Inc.
42 Broadway, New York, N.Y. 10004
(212) 269–9236

Castle Convertible Fund, Inc.
75 Maiden Lane, New York, N.Y. 10038
(212) 480–0500

LOAD MUTUAL FUNDS

American Capital Harbor Fund, Inc.
2777 Allen Parkway, Houston, Texas 77019
(713) 522–1111

Convertible Yield Securities, Inc.
Eleven Greenway Plaza, Houston, Texas 77046
(713) 626–1919

Phoenix Convertible Fund
One American Row, Hartford, Ct. 06115
(800) 243–1574

Putnam Convertible Fund
One Post Office Square, Boston, Mass. 02109
(617) 292–1000

NO-LOAD MUTUAL FUNDS

Noddings-Calamos Convertible Income Fund
2001 Spring Road, Oak Brook, Illinois, 60521
(800) 251–2411 outside Illinois
(800) 821–6458 within Illinois

Noddings-Calamos Convertible Growth Fund
2001 Spring Road, Oak Brook, Illinois, 60521
(800) 251–2411 outside Illinois
(800) 821–6458 within Illinois

NOTES FOR CHAPTER 11

1. American Association of Individual Investors (AAII)
612 North Michigan Avenue
Chicago, Illinois 60611
"The American Association of Individual Investors is an independent, non-profit corporation formed for the purpose of assisting individuals in becoming effective managers of their own assets through programs of education, information and research." —quoted from the AAII's monthly journal.
2. National Association of Personal Financial Advisors (NAPFA)
3726-J Olentangy River Road
Columbus, Ohio 43214

CHAPTER 12

Building Wealth Systematically and Unemotionally

Investors work at building wealth for two basic reasons. One is to assure the continuance of the lifestyle enjoyed before retirement. The other is to leave an estate to one's heirs. Let's assume your goals include both objectives; how much wealth is enough?

The answer will vary depending on your individual needs. Suppose that after a successful career, you enter retirement years with investable assets totaling a magical one million dollars, free from income tax obligations (e.g. an after-tax lump-sum distribution from your company's profit sharing plan plus your personal investments). How should you invest the million dollars? Will your choice accomplish your objectives?

INVESTING IN RETIREMENT

There are numerous investment alternatives from which to select. A popular choice for many people entering retirement is an annuity, but that idea should be quickly rejected. Although an annuity will provide fixed income for life, nothing will be left for your estate. Next, you would probably consider long-term government or corporate bonds, tax-exempt municipals, and short-term money market instruments. Because you are both uncertain about interest rate trends and acutely aware of the miserable bond market performance in recent years, let's assume you opt for the safety and liquidity of U.S. government Treasury bills. If you do make T-bills your ongoing investment strategy, will you be able to meet your dual objectives: a comfortable income and a sizable future estate?

To simplify the arithmetic, let's assume you receive a constant 10 percent T-bill rate of return over the next 20 years, and experience a 10 percent inflation rate (remember from Chapter 1 that T-bills just kept pace with inflation in the past). Let's also assume that all interest earned will be taxed at 40 percent, based on today's 50 percent *maximum* rate. (The maximum reached 91 percent during the 50s and has been as high as 70 percent for "unearned" income in recent years; there are no guarantees that future administrations will not raise it back to the 70 percent level, or higher.) State and local income taxes are not included in the calculations since they vary widely, but the 40 percent tax-rate assumption is on the high side for present federal taxes and should thus cover additional state and local taxes for most people.

At a 10 percent T-bill rate, you will receive $100,000 pre-tax interest, leaving $60,000 available for spending after taxes. Although you may not require this much in addition to Social Security payments, Table

Table 12–1. Investing $1,000,000 in retirement—original strategy

Assumptions
* Investment strategy: buy Treasury bills at 10 percent interest
* Inflation is 10 percent
* Interest earned is taxed at 40 percent
* All earnings are spend each year

	Years into Retirement		
	0	*10*	*20*
Investment capital			
Investment in T-bills	$1,000,000	$1,000,000	$1,000,000
Adjusted for inflation	$1,000,000	$ 390,000	$ 150,000
Annual earnings			
Pre-tax interest earned	$ 100,000	$ 100,000	$ 100,000
Taxes	$ 40,000	$ 40,000	$ 40,000
After-tax earnings	$ 60,000	$ 60,000	$ 60,000
Earnings reinvested	$ 0	$ 0	$ 0
Earnings spent	$ 60,000	$ 60,000	$ 60,000
Purchasing power	$ 60,000	$ 23,000	$ 8,900

12–1 shows what will happen if you set your life-style at this income level.

The calculations of Table 12–1 show that at the end of ten years, your capital's *value* will have dropped from $1 million to $390,000, and your annual purchasing power will have declined from the first year's $60,000 to $23,000. At the end of twenty years, the numbers are $150,000 and $8,900. Is $150,000 what you had in mind when you originally intended to leave a sizable estate? Will you be able to live off $8,900? What will happen if your life span exceeds twenty years, or if you experience a serious uninsured illness? What will happen if future inflation goes above 10 percent? These are the kinds of problems you don't want in your retirement years.

The shocking truth is that future inflation, and taxes paid on inflated earnings, may destroy *both* your wealth and your standard of living. How many retired people, who applaud higher Social Security and other deficit-building government "benefits," are aware that the resulting inflation is destroying their *other* dollar assets: their fixed-income investments, their non-indexed pensions, their annuities?

Recognizing the frightening implications of the analysis, your only choice is to *both* cut back drastically your intended life-style and to increase substantially the earning power of your investment capital (i.e., assume the risks associated with high-performance investing). The first portion of that "choice" is analyzed by Table 12–2.

The analysis of Table 12–2 shows what will happen if you remain in T-bills and spend *only half* the after-tax earnings ($30,000 in the first year instead of $60,000, for example), while reinvesting the remaining half, equal to 3 percent of your investment capital, each year. You will thus be adding to your capital base every year, which will lead to additional earnings above the $60,000 starting level in future years. While improving the long-term outlook somewhat and increasing your pre-inflation-adjusted investment capital and earnings each year, this approach still falls far short of your original goals. At the end of twenty years, your capital, having a nominal value of $1,800,000, is worth only $270,000 and your annual purchasing power is down to $8,000. Even if you reinvest *all* earnings and live off other resources, your estate's value will drop to less than half in twenty years. The reinvestment of *after-tax* earnings from "risk-free" T-bills cannot be expected to keep pace with inflation. You must also increase your capital's earning power.

High-performance investing, with emphasis on long-term capital gains

Table 12–2. Investing $1,000,000 in retirement—alternative strategy

Assumptions
* Investment strategy: buy Treasury bills at 10 percent interest
* Inflation is 10 percent
* Interest earned is taxed at 40 percent
* 50 percent of after-tax earnings are spent each year
* 50 percent of after-tax earnings are reinvested each year

	Years into Retirement		
	0	*10*	*20*
Investment capital			
Investment in T-bills	$1,000,000	$1,340,000	$1,800,000
Adjusted for inflation	$1,000,000	$ 520,000	$ 270,000
Annual earnings			
Pre-tax interest earned	$ 100,000	$ 134,000	$ 180,000
Taxes	$ 40,000	$ 54,000	$ 72,000
After-tax earnings	$ 60,000	$ 80,000	$ 108,000
Earnings reinvested	$ 30,000	$ 40,000	$ 54,000
Earnings spent	$ 30,000	$ 40,000	$ 54,000
Purchasing power	$ 30,000	$ 15,000	$ 8,000

for tax reduction, will probably give you many sleepless nights (every bear market) during your retirement years. Although I dislike being the bearer of bad tidings, these problems would probably be dwarfed by the anxieties you could expect to face if you attempted to live on fixed income in an inflationary environment. A million-dollar nest egg is simply not enough to assure worry-free retirement at anywhere near the living standards you may have envisioned. It will certainly not give you the estate you had hoped for.

My analysis made certain assumptions about inflation and interest rates. Although based on historical relationships, they might miss the real world of the future by a wide mark. I have no crystal ball. Perhaps inflation will continue to subside and risk-free investments will provide high real returns (before taxes, maybe; after taxes, highly unlikely). We have experienced both waning inflation and real pre-tax money market returns in recent years, for the first time since the Great Depression. Can we count on these trends to continue through your retirement? Possibly, but I would not want to plan on it. Rather, I believe, you should try to protect yourself by anticipating all possible outcomes, including both extremes: higher inflation rates *or* deflation. If you can guard against the extremes, you can enjoy your retirement years as you planned.

A SUPERIOR STRATEGY FOR INVESTING IN RETIREMENT

Table 12–3 illustrates high-performance investing coupled with spending restraints, $30,000 in the first year, as in Table 12–2. This alternative strategy assumes a 6 percent total return on investment *above* Treasury bills, in line with the additional returns achieved by the stock market in the past. Of the 16 percent total return, based on 10 percent T-bills, I assume fully taxable income at 6 percent and long-term capital gains (taken each year for tax-calculation purposes) at 10 percent. As a consequence, your standard of living starts at the same level as in Table 12–2, but you have substantially greater after-tax earnings to reinvest (9 percent versus 3 percent). Each year's 9 percent addition to your investment account nearly keeps pace with the 10 percent inflation rate. Thus, both your capital base and your future purchasing power are not as seriously eroded as in Tables 12–1 and 12–2.

BUILDING WEALTH

I hope my examples will help convince those in retirement of the need for *high-performance* investing. The examples should also jolt into action those in the process of preparing for retirement. Younger investors should realize that they will probably require a much larger retirement nest egg than they are presently planning.

The average person has at his disposal two basic ways to build wealth, and *both* are equally important. First, invest regularly, especially in tax-sheltered programs such as your company's pension or profit sharing plans and your personal IRA. Second, invest wisely, by searching out superior, if not popular, strategies.

The need to add funds periodically to your investment portfolio should be obvious. My only comment on this point is to urge you to put aside

Table 12–3. Investing $1,000,000 in retirement—best strategy

Assumptions
* Investment strategy: buy securities yielding 6 percent plus 10 percent growth
* Inflation is 10 percent
* Yield is taxed at 40 percent and long-term capital gains are taxed at 16 percent
* 25 percent of after-tax earnings are spent each year
* 75 percent of after-tax earnings are reinvested each year

	Years into Retirement		
	0	*10*	*20*
Investment capital			
Investment in securities	$1,000,000	$2,370,000	$5,600,000
Adjusted for inflation	$1,000,000	$ 910,000	$ 830,000
Annual earnings			
Yield	$ 60,000	$ 142,000	$ 336,000
Long-term capital gains	100,000	237,000	560,000
Total pre-tax return	$ 160,000	$ 379,000	$ 896,000
Taxes	$ 40,000	$ 95,000	$ 224,000
After-tax earnings	$ 120,000	$ 284,000	$ 672,000
Earnings reinvested	$ 90,000	$ 213,000	$ 504,000
Earnings spent	$ 30,000	$ 71,000	$ 168,000
Purchasing power	$ 30,000	$ 27,000	$ 25,000

as much as possible and as early as possible. Do not wait until you are 50 or older before planning for retirement if you can possibly begin earlier. Remember, $2,000 per year for 40 years in an Individual Retirement Account *can* grow to a *real* million dollars (i.e., earnings at 10 percent per year *above the rate of inflation*). But recognize that your IRA's final value will be fully taxable. It will not be free from income tax obligations as I assumed in the examples. Thus, you should supplement your IRA with other investment programs.

Your company's pension plan is another excellent source for building wealth, providing it permits you to take a lump-sum distribution upon retirement. Unfortunately, most large corporate plans convert your vested interest into an insurance company annuity without giving you a choice. While the fixed income may look great at first, inflation can quickly destroy its real value, and an annuity leaves nothing to your estate. Small business owners can design carefully-structured pension or profit-sharing plans. If you own a company and have not yet implemented one or both of these plans, get in touch with your accountant and/or your attorney.

Once you have done everything possible to put aside as much as you can in one or more of the above tax-advantaged accounts, the next step is to determine your investment strategy. This book details a number of superior strategies for achieving above average rates of return. But unless you truly understand the merits of convertible securities, you may succumb to the more conventional modes of investing—those recommended by your accountant, your attorney, your banker, your insurance agent, or your stockbroker. These professional advisors will seldom put their stamp of approval on anything out of the ordinary, and they will probably not read, let alone study, this book if you hand it to them. Their primary concern is to play it safe, since they have nothing to gain and everything to lose by recommending unpopular investments. There is an unwritten tenet followed by the play-it-safe advisors: "It is acceptable to lose money for a client in utility stocks or government bonds, but *never* lose money (even over short periods of time) in a strategy the client does not understand."

Let's examine two of today's stock market strategies that you might consider for a high-performance investment program: blue chip growth stocks and small company stocks.

BLUE CHIP GROWTH STOCKS

Suppose that in 1973 you received the following ten year forecasts for XYZ Corp., the premier company in a dynamically growing industry.

Sales growth	250%
Earnings growth	250%
Dividend growth	230%

Let's further assume that over the ten year period these vital financial statistics were achieved via unfaltering year-to-year increases. A true corporate success story? *YES!* A sure path to stock market riches? Unfortunately, *NO!*

Replace the letters XYZ with IBM and enter the real world of investing. Exhibit 12–1 graphs the annual highs and lows for IBM's common stock over the ten-year period. Beginning with an average price of $75 in 1973, IBM dropped to below $40 in 1974, rebounded to about $80 in 1979 and sank to below $50 in 1981, the eighth year after purchase. It wasn't until the ninth year, 1982, that the stock moved decisively above the $75 purchase price, reaching an all-time high of $134 in 1983. Until the long awaited upside breakout, the only return investors received over eight years was the cash dividend, from a low 1.5 percent in 1973 to 4.4 percent in 1982, minuscule returns from America's number one growth company. How many early investors had the patience to stay with IBM through those disappointing years until its dramatic advance beginning in August 1982?

Despite the 1982–83 rally, IBM's ten-year advance, from an average

Exhibit 12–1. Annual price data for IBM's common stock, 1973–1983

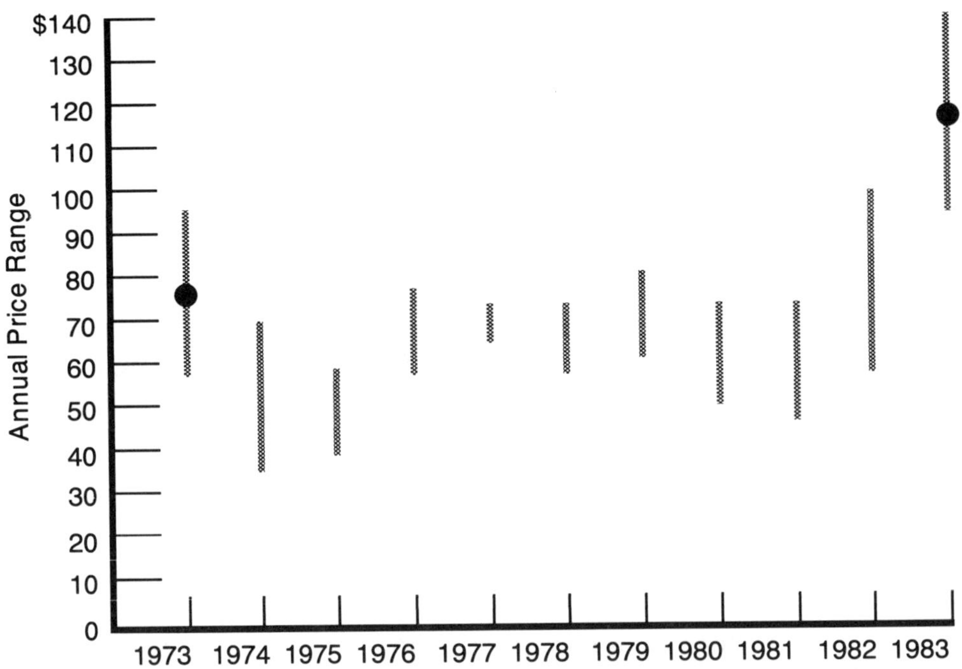

price of $75 in 1973 to an average of $113 in 1983, was only 50 percent. Assuming dividend reinvestment, the annualized pre-tax return works out to less than 8 percent (T-bills returned nearly 9 percent). While I expect most IBM holders were not happy with these results, other large growth stocks did much worse. A sample of five institutional money management favorites is presented in Table 12–4: Avon Products, Eastman Kodak, IBM, Sears, and Xerox. Of the five, only IBM turned in a gain for the ten years; the average for the five stocks was nearly *a 40 percent loss.* Note that in all cases, these large growth companies in 1973 became much larger ten years later as shown under the columns titled "book value." These were all successful companies. What went wrong?

Back in the early 70s, these corporate success stories were considered to be "one decision" stocks by the banks and other institutional money managers. They believed that these stocks could be bought at any price, since future earnings would more than make up for the high price/earnings multiples of the time. From the table, the p/e ratios for the five averaged 34 in 1973; in 1983 the average p/e was a more realistic 14 (or 11.5 if we exclude Eastman Kodak's 22 p/e). Their average dividend yield was 1.3 percent in 1973; in 1983 it was 5.2. It's easy for us to look back and say what a lousy job the money managers did by paying such high prices for future earnings, but that was the financial community's *consensus* at the time. The big growth stocks were *faddish,* just like conglomerates in the late 60s, energy stocks in 1979–80, and small high-

Table 12–4. Performance data for selected large growth stocks, 1973–1983

	Average Stock Price		*Price/ Earnings Ratios*		*Book Value $ Millions*	
	1973	*1983*	*1973*	*1983*	*1973*	*1983*
Avon Products	$ 99	$ 29	48	13	447	1,204
Eastman Kodak	$128	$ 78	33	22	3,118	7,542
IBM	$ 75	$113	28	13	8,814	23,220
Sears	$ 50	$ 36	22	10	4,992	9,786
Xerox	$142	$ 44	39	10	1,496	4,222
Averages	$ 99	$ 60	34	14		

Source: *The Value Line Investment Survey.* Copyright 1984, Value Line, Inc.

tech stocks in more recent years. One sure way to lose money in the markets is to chase the latest fad. Unfortunately, that is precisely what people do when they "play it safe" with currently popular investments.

Today, high quality, low p/e growth companies appear to be reasonably priced and should probably be viewed as the core holdings for most common stock portfolios. They should give future investors the stock market performance they seek without exposing their portfolios to unacceptable risks. As a superior alternative, *low-risk convertible bonds* should provide higher returns, at less volatility, than these blue chip common stocks. The convertible bond market is the best choice for knowledegable investors.

SMALL COMPANY STOCKS

Much has been written in recent years about the performance of smaller company stocks compared with the blue chips. Exhibit 12–2 shows how the stocks making up the fifth (smallest) quintile on the New York Stock Exchange performed relative to other modes of investing. Between 1926 and 1981, a dollar invested in the small stock category would have grown to $597 versus $133 for the S&P 500.

Be aware, however, that these small capitalization stocks were not all emerging growth companies, newly listed on the big board. Many were "fallen angels" which *dropped* into the lowest twenty percent category. As I have stressed repeatedly, the best market opportunities are in the non-institutional areas. When companies fall on hard times, institutions do not want to show them in their client portfolios quarter after quarter. Thus, institutional selling pressure creates bargains for smaller investors.

As long as the institutions continue to dominate the markets, these bargains should continue to become available. The graphs of Exhibit 12–2 clearly illustrate this point. Most of the advantage gained by the smaller companies occurred since the 1974 bear market, a period that experienced ever-increasing domination of the market by institutions. Therefore, I don't believe these small company stocks are faddish just because they have performed well in recent years.

High price-volatility is the biggest problem when dealing with low-quality stocks. It demands nerves of steel, a trait unlikely to be found in most conservative investors. For those interested in this extra-high-

Exhibit 12–2. Wealth indices of investments in the U.S. capital markets, 1926–81

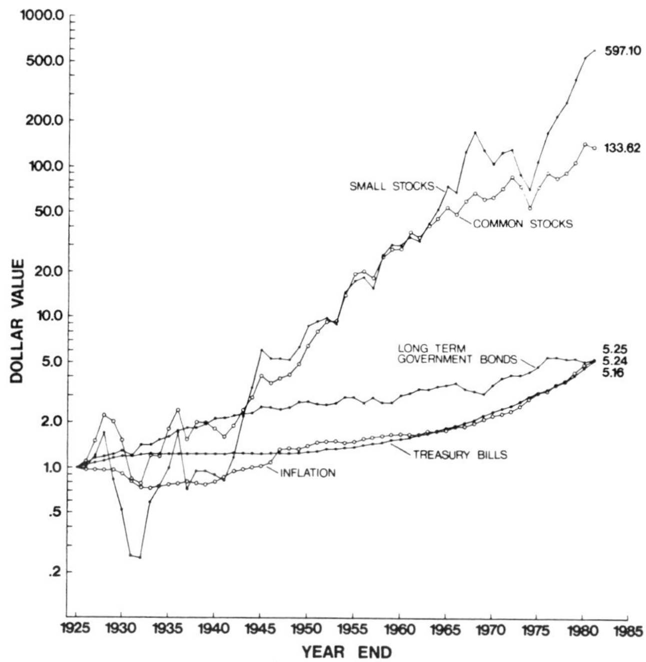

Source: Roger G. Ibbotson and Rex A. Sinquefield, *Stocks, Bonds, Bills and Inflation: The Past and the Future,* 1982 ed. (Charlottesville, Va.: The Financial Analysts Research Foundation, 1982.)

performance market sector, I strongly urge the *aggressive convertible-bond alternative.* Undervalued convertibles of secondary companies should continue to outperform their higher-risk stocks, at less volatility. Once again, the convertible bond market is the best choice for knowledgeable investors.

SOME FINAL THOUGHTS

The financial markets offer a wide variety of instruments and strategies. Most are good, a few are exceptional, and some are sure losers. As an individual investor or as a trustee for a pension or profit sharing plan, you must acquire the knowledge and skills necessary for sorting through the innumerable alternatives. You should choose only those that offer above-average performance and that best fit your objectives. The fact that you are a reader of serious financial books places you far ahead of the typical investor, as well as most advisors others might turn to for guidance.

As a knowledgeable investor, however, you run the risk of getting too close to the markets, a statement I do not make lightly. Over the years, many of my more sophisticated clients have tended to become far too involved. Their weekly or monthly scrutiny has often led to bad decisions as they added money at market tops, only to become discouraged at market bottoms. Our firm's best-performing clients have been those who are unemotional and long-term oriented; an occasional meeting or telephone conversation is usually sufficient for updating progress and for future planning. Those who monitor their progress too frequently seldom have the patience to let time work to their advantage.

Therefore, I *strongly* urge you to set your sights for the *long term.* Recognize that any investment strategy, even attractive convertibles, will underperform your expectations from time to time. *No strategy is perfect.* Know also that all investment strategies go through market cycles. You must have the patience to ride through the down phases if you expect to build wealth. There is no way to get out at the top and back in at the bottom. *Professional money managers can't do it. You can't do it!* Market timing receives far too much undeserved attention by the financial media; it doesn't work and it wrongly encourages investors to jump in and out. It can lead only to unnecessary costs and poor performance.

Finally, I urge you to concentrate your time and attention on selecting *market strategies,* not on picking individual securities. I'm told, for example, that it takes a skilled financial analyst three days to get a firm grasp on most annual reports. Do you have the time (and ability) to do this yourself, as well as to study the many other factors that must be considered when making specific security selections? If not, you should hire professional managers to implement your chosen strategies. Many no-load mutual funds, as well as certain investment advisors for larger portfolios, do provide professional money management at bargain prices.

Special Investment Situations

In Chapter 3, I mentioned that there exist a number of "non-standard" investment instruments that offer either greater opportunities for alert investors or hidden traps for the unwary. This appendix describes several such instruments. All are special convertible securities which I have used in the past. Other non-standard instruments have also existed, and still others will surely appear in the future. Some are bound to be radically different, for corporate treasurers are constantly stretching their imaginations for novel, salable ways to raise new financing.

Let me stress here that all convertibles, both conventional and special, may contain unusual terms requiring *very careful* consideration. Such terms have more than once handed investors abnormal price changes due to unexpected market conditions.

Plus-cash convertible. This security requires an additional cash payment on conversion. Since the extra cash requirement is constant, regardless of the common stock's market price, the conversion value changes more rapidly than the price of the underlying stock. This type of special convertible may appeal to investors seeking greater leverage than that offered by conventional convertibles.

An example was the United Air Lines 4.25s of 1992, exchangeable for 19 common shares upon payment of $260 until 7–1–82, at which time the conversion privilege expired. With the common stock at $20 in 1981, the bond's conversion value was only $120, calculated as follows:

$$
\begin{aligned}
\text{Conversion} &= 19 \text{ shares} \times \$20 \text{ per share} - \$260 \\
&= \$380 - \$260 \\
&= \$120
\end{aligned}
$$

If the common stock doubled to $40, the conversion value would increase by 317 percent to $500.

$$
\begin{aligned}
\text{Conversion value} &= 19 \text{ shares} \times \$40 \text{ per share} - \$260 \\
&= \$760 - \$260 \\
&= \$500
\end{aligned}
$$

Unit convertible. A "unit convertible" security is not exchangeable only for common stock, but for a "unit," a package of one or more securities that may or may not include the common. The evaluation of this convertible requires additional work, but a unit convertible is potentially more rewarding since the marketplace may have extra difficulty assigning it a fair value.

One example of a recently attractive unit convertible, the LTV $5.25 convertible preferred, is convertible into one unit consisting of 3.92 shares of LTV common stock and 0.78 shares of LTV's $1.25 convertible preferred. These terms resulted from LTV's acquisition of Republic Steel in 1984.

Indirect convertible. This security may be exchanged for common stock via another convertible. For example, the Instrument Systems 12s of 1999 were each convertible into 90 shares of a preferred stock, which in turn was convertible into 10 shares of common. Since the preferred paid a very small dividend, its price action was directly related to the common. The bond was therefore evaluated as being convertible into 900 shares of common stock. Other indirect convertibles may require greater study when evaluating their risk-reward characteristics.

Fabricated convertible. This special convertible is a combination of warrants plus straight bonds that may be used (at par value) in lieu of cash when exercising the warrants. To determine the number of warrants that should be purchased with each straight bond, simply divide the $1,000 par value of the bond by the exercise price of the warrant. The combination results in risk-reward characteristics similar to conventional convertibles, yet it provides greater portfolio-management flexibility since the bonds and warrants are traded separately. This was a popular form of financing in the 60s, when warrants were in vogue. Its popularity declined during the 70s, but warrants are regaining favor.

A recent issue was brought to the market by MCI Communications. Their 9.5s of 1993 straight bonds are usable when exercising their warrants that expire in August 1988. To fabricate an MCI convertible the investor should purchase 36 warrants along with each bond ($1,000 ÷ $27.50 warrant exercise price = 36.4 warrants).

Synthetic convertible. Combining call options (or warrants) with money market instruments creates synthetic convertible securities. This technique can be a profitable alternative to owning common stock when short-term interest rates are high and calls are undervalued. By placing most of the investment capital in high-yielding money market instruments and the small balance in call options, the synthetic convertible may offer stock market opportunity at a lower risk level than owning common stocks. Some investors, for example, routinely buy calls with 10 percent of their funds while holding 90 percent in the money markets.

Delayed convertible. This convertible, which gets its name from its conversion features, generally sells at a discount below its future conversion value. A delayed convertible will usually fall into one of two categories:

1. A convertible with fixed conversion terms that specify the number of common stock shares to be received, commencing on a specified future date.
2. A convertible exchangeable into common stock beginning on a specified date with the conversion ratio based on a formula dependent on the future price of the common.

Convertible exchangeable preferred stock. This convertible preferred can be redeemed at the option of the company in exchange for convertible bonds of the company.

Changes in terms. Some convertibles have fixed schedules for changing their conversion terms at future specified dates. These changes usually involve a reduction of the conversion ratio, which can depress the convertible's price as the date nears.

The Pennsylvania REIT 9.75s of 2003, for example, will experience an abrupt reduction of their conversion ratio from 39.215 shares to 35.211 shares on August 1, 1988. Depending on the bond's price at that time, conversion may be necessary to avoid a significant loss of value. If the bond was trading at its conversion value of 150, for example, it would drop to about 135. Conversion terms can also change unexpectedly. Some companies will announce a temporary increase of the conversion ratio to encourage immediate conversion.

Expiration of conversion privileges. Even more dangerous than a modest reduction of the conversion ratio is the scheduled termination of all conversion privileges. In this event, the convertible's market price immediately drops to its investment value as it became a nonconvertible bond.

Recent examples include the American Airlines 5.25s of 1998, whose conversion privileges terminated 12–15–83, and the United Air Lines 4.25s of 1992, which terminated 7–1–82. Trading at large conversion premiums at the time, both convertibles declined to their investment values of about $500 as the termination dates neared.

Call provisions. Practically all convertible bonds, and most convertible preferreds, may be called (retired) by the company just as straight bonds and preferreds. The call price for bonds is usually a few points over face value (e.g., 105). Companies that issue convertibles generally will redeem them when, owing to a significant common stock price advance, the convertible is trading well above par (e.g. 130 to 150). If a convertible is subject to being called in the near future, be careful not to pay a premium over its conversion value; when called, the convertible will immediately drop to its conversion value and the premium will be lost.

Companies normally do not call convertibles with the intention of redeeming them for cash. Their usual objective is to force conversion into common stock to improve their balance sheet, or to reduce their tax liabilities if the common stock is a low dividend payer. The company must therefore be cautious in timing the call because subsequent market action by the common might force them to come up with cash they may not have. For example, if a bond's call price was 105 and it was trading with a 110 conversion value, the company would probably not issue a call because a small price decline by its common at any time up to the call date (usually a 30 day notice must be given) could reduce the conversion value to below the call price. Bondholders would then tender for cash rather than convert.

Companies will often call a bond just prior to its interest payment date and save a considerable amount of interest. The accrued interest must be added to the call price, but interest is not received by the bondholders if they convert. For this reason, convertible bonds will trade at a discount below conversion value, when called, to reflect the loss of accrued interest. The accrued interest is added to the purchase price if the bond is sold, but the new owner will not recover it when the bond is converted; hence the discount.

Antidilution provisions. Convertibles are almost always protected against stock splits, stock dividends, and the like via an appropriate increase in their conversion ratios. However, there have been instances where a company has spun off a subsidiary to stockholders without adjusting the terms of its convertibles. Thus, the convertible bond or preferred becomes exchangeable into the same number of shares as before, but the common stock could be worth considerably less.

Sinking fund convertibles. Some convertible bonds and preferreds have sinking fund provisions that retire much of the issue prior to its maturity date. Once the sinking fund redemptions begin, the convertible will start to behave like a short-term bond nearing its maturity date.

Other convertibles may have characteristics that are similar to a sinking fund. The Georgia Pacific $2.24 A preferred, for example, is scheduled to be redeemed at $39 over a five year period which started April 1, 1984. However, the company may choose not to redeem, in which event it must increase the preferred's annual dividend to $4.00.

Preferreds in arrears. Most companies are required to pay omitted past dividends on their preferred stocks before paying any future common stock dividends. These *cumulative* preferreds can build up very large dividend arrearages over a period of years and thus offer the potential for large payouts if the company regains profitability.

Tender offers for discounted bonds. Bonds are carried on a corporation's books as a liability at full par value. To improve its balance sheet, a company may make a cash tender or some other exchange offer for its deep-discounted bonds. The value offered is usually well above the bond's current market price to assure a favorable response.

Mergers and tender offers for common stock. These events may have either positive or negative impact on a convertible's market value, depending on the specific terms of the package offered to the common shareholders and the convertible's premium over conversion value.

The most dangerous and unfair situation occurs when a company is acquired for low-volatility securities (e.g., straight bonds or preferreds) or cash. To a large extent, the conversion premium reflects the possibility that the underlying common stock may make a meaningful price advance sometime during the convertible's lifetime. In the event of a takeover, convertibles are normally protected to the extent that they will receive the same package as the stockholders. When common stock of the acquiring company is received in a merger, for example, it would be considered fair compensation because the convertible then becomes exchangeable for the new common. However, if cash or low-volatility securities are received, the convertible could be adversely affected. I have seen some discounted convertible bonds become "straight" bonds, for all practical purposes, as they can only be converted into cash having a value below the convertible's investment floor.

These are some of the pluses and minuses I have experienced in working with convertible securities. There will certainly be new and different ones in the future. Through careful attention to detail, alert investors should be able to avoid most traps and to profit from the unusual opportunities that often arise.

Since unexpected events may occur, I recommend that investors keep their securities in street name at a brokerage firm, rather than in their safety deposit boxes. Brokerage firms are alert to these unusual happenings and send notices when action is necessary.

An Evaluation of Interest Rate Risk for Convertible Bonds

The assumption that long-term interest rates would not change in the near term made it possible to evaluate various convertible strategies with relatively simple graphs and simple arithmetic. However, interest rates do fluctuate. It is thus important to understand the potential impact of interest rate changes on convertibles as well as on traditional strategies employing fixed-income securities.

Exhibit B–1 repeats the convertible price curve for High-Tech Industries 10s of 2004 (Exhibit 4–1, page 38) trading at par, with long-term interest rates at 16 percent. Exhibit B–2 illustrates expected new price curves should interest rates rise to 20 percent or drop to 12 percent. For stock price changes of −50, 0 and +100 percent, the estimated bond prices are as follows:

	Estimated Convertible Bond Price for Stock Price Changes of:		
Long-Term Interest Rates	*−50 Percent*	*0 Percent*	*+100 Percent*
12 percent	90	106	160
16 percent	78	100	160
20 percent	69	95	160

Exhibit B–1. The convertible price curve: High-Tech Industries 10 percent, 20-year bond (conversion ratio = 40 shares, straight bond equivalent yield = 16 percent)

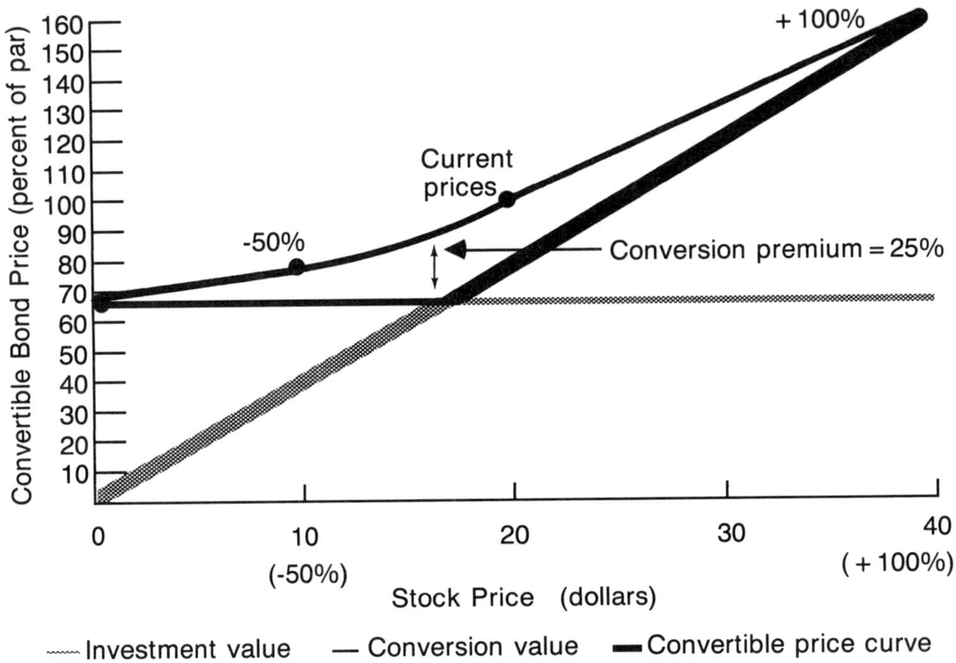

As shown by the price curves, interest rate fluctuations would have little influence on the convertible's price if its stock advanced; upside prices are controlled by the conversion value line, which cannot change. If the stock declined, a higher investment value would moderate the bond's price drop, or a lower investment value would cause a greater decline.

PERFORMANCE EVALUATION

Table B–1 repeats the risk-reward analysis for the High-Tech bond compared to the traditional balanced approach (Table 4–2, page 40).

Exhibit B–2. Convertible price curves: High-Tech Industries 10 percent, 20-year bond (conversion ratio = 40 shares, straight bond equivalent yield = 12 percent or 20 percent)

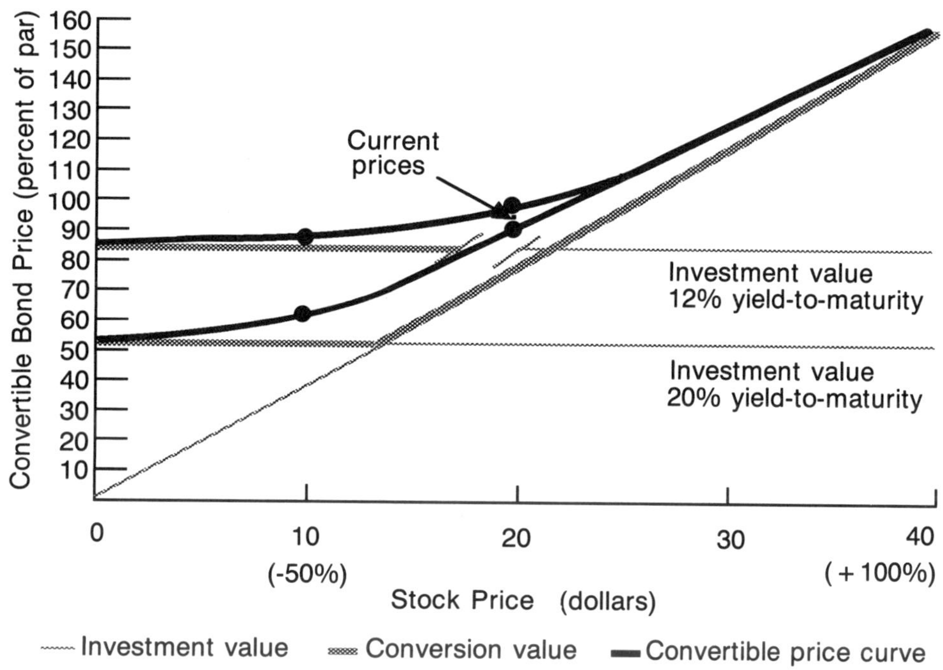

Table B–1. Risk-reward analysis: High-Tech Industries 10s of 2004 at 100 versus common stock at $20 and straight bonds at 16 percent

	Stock Price Change in 12 Months		
	−50 Percent	*0 Percent*	*+100 Percent*
Balanced approach			
Common stock	−50%	0%	+100%
Straight bonds	+16	+16	+ 16
50% stock/50% bonds	−17%	+ 8%	+ 58%
Convertible bond			
Capital gain or loss	−22%	0%	+ 60%
Interest received	+10	+10	+ 10
Total return	−12%	+10%	+ 70%
Convertible advantage	+ 5%	+ 2%	+ 12%

Tables B–2 and B–3 present new risk-reward calculations for interest rates of 20 percent and 12 percent. *Study* these calculations and the accompanying conclusions carefully. Pay particular attention to how performance comparisons between the convertible bond and the balanced approach can sharply diverge. They help to explain why the Noddings-Calamos low-risk convertible securities index (Chapter 8) did so much better than the balanced approach during its early years when interest rates were steadily rising and why it substantially underperformed when interest rates plummeted in 1982. Both divergences were quite understandable, given the actual events that unfolded in the stock and straight bond markets.

There are nine possible scenarios for stock/bond combination portfolios based on the specific price action of each security type:

Stocks	*Bonds*	*Better Performer*
sideways	sideways	Convertibles
sideways	rising	Balanced approach
sideways	falling	Convertibles
rising	sideways	Convertibles
rising	rising	Balanced approach
rising	falling	Convertibles, by far
falling	sideways	Convertibles
falling	rising	Convertibles
falling	falling	Convertibles

As shown by Tables B–1, B–2, and B–3 (summarized above), undervalued convertibles should modestly outperform the balanced approach most of the time. During these six different market scenarios, a convertible portfolio's performance can reasonably be compared to traditional balanced-approach investing. The other three scenarios will cause even most professionals to "throw up their hands in despair" when it comes to evaluating short-term performance results.

Table B–2. Risk-reward analysis: High-Tech Industries 10s of 2004 at 100 versus common stock at $20 and straight bonds at 16 percent, assuming interest rates rise to 20 percent in one year

	Stock Price Change in 12 Months		
	−50 Percent	*0 Percent*	*+100 Percent*
Balanced approach			
Common stock	−50%	0%	+100%
Straight bonds			
Capital loss*	−20%	−20%	− 20%
Interest received	+16	+16	+16
Total return	− 4%	− 4%	− 4%
50% stock/50% bonds	−27%	− 2%	+ 48%
Convertible bond			
Capital gain or loss	−31%	− 5%	+ 60%
Interest received	+10	+10	+ 10
Total return	−21%	+ 5%	+ 70%
Convertible advantage	+ 6%	+ 7%	+ 22%

* A 16 percent bond purchased at 100 will drop to about 80 if interest rates rise to 20 percent.

CONCLUSIONS

1. Rising interest rates will result in greater losses for both the convertible bond and the balanced approach if the common stock declines. The convertible, however, will retain its advantage over the balanced approach (−21 percent versus −27 percent).
2. If the common stock remains unchanged, the convertible will move modestly lower but will outperform the balanced approach by an even greater margin (+5 percent versus −2 percent).
3. If the common doubles, the convertible will provide the same total return as in a steady interest rate environment (+70 percent) and will significantly outperform the balanced approach; its advantage increases from +12 percent (Table B–1) to +22 percent.

Table B–3. Risk-reward analysis: High-Tech Industries 10s of 2004 at 100 versus common stock at $20 and straight bonds at 16 percent, assuming interest rates decline to 12 percent in one year.

	Stock Price Change in 12 Months		
	−50 Percent	*0 Percent*	*+100 Percent*
Balanced approach			
Common stock	−50%	0%	+100%
Straight bonds			
Capital gain*	+30%	+30%	+ 30%
Interest received	+16	+16	+ 16
Total return	+46%	+46%	+ 46%
50% stock/50% bonds	− 2%	+23%	+ 73%
Convertible bond			
Captial gain or loss	−10%	+ 6%	+ 60%
Interest received	+10	+10	+ 10
Total return	0%	+16%	+ 70%
Convertible advantage	+ 2%	− 7%	− 3%

* A 16 percent bond purchased at 100 will rise to about 130 if interest rates decline to 12 percent.

CONCLUSIONS

1. Falling interest rates will cushion losses for both the convertible and the balanced approach if the common stock declines. The convertible will lose some of its advantage (0 percent versus −2 percent) at a 50 percent stock decline.
2. If the common stock remains unchanged, the convertible will move modestly higher but will underperform the balanced approach (+16 percent versus +23 percent).
3. If the common doubles, the convertible will provide the same return as in a steady interest rate environment (+70 percent) but the balanced approach will do much better (+73 percent compared to +58 percent from Table B–1).

Closing A Convertible Position via the Conversion Process

The limited liquidity for convertible securities works to the investor's advantage since institutional money managers are forced to use the larger markets in stocks and straight bonds. This helps to create undervalued opportunities like those illustrated throughout this book, but it also means that at times a necessary order execution at a fair price may simply be impossible. There are ways to deal with this problem.

Convertible positions are usually closed out after a significant price advance, at which time the convertible is no longer an attractive low-risk alternative to its common stock. However, if the convertible is not actively traded, the best bid may be below its conversion value. Rather than sell at a discount, the most cost-effective method for closing the position often will be to exchange the convertible for common stock and sell the more actively traded common. In actual practice, the common stock usually is sold first, and the stock received later via the conversion process is used to offset the earlier sale.

When considering close out via the conversion process, here are the major factors to consider:

1. Accrued interest is lost when a bond is converted.
2. The capital to carry the position during the conversion period (usually about four weeks) will not be earning any return (90 percent may be released for other investments, but margin interest will be charged on the resulting debit balance).

3. Dividends must be paid if the stock declares a dividend during the conversion period and the record date falls within that conversion period.
4. Brokerage commissions will differ and should therefore be taken into account.

To illustrate these points, consider the High-Tech Industries 10s of 2004. Assume the common stock has risen to $40 per share on May 1 and a 10 bond position (equal to 400 shares) is to be closed out. At $40, the bond's conversion value is 160 ($40 × 40 shares = $1,600) but the best bid is only 155. Assume the bond pays its semiannual interest on June 1 ($50 for each bond) and the common stock declares a $.10 per share dividend to record holders as of May 10 (ex-dividend date is May 3).

Three possible courses of action should be considered: immediate bond sale at 155, sell 400 shares and convert immediately, or sell 400 shares and convert after the June 1 interest date. The arithmetic for evaluating these alternatives is shown in Table C–1.

Table C–1. Alternate methods for closing a convertible position

Immediate bond sale	
Sell 10 bonds at 155	= $15,500
Accrued bond interest for five months	= 416
Commissions	= (100)
Net proceeds on settlement date in one week	= $15,816
Sell 400 shares and convert immediately	
Sell 400 common stock at $40	= $16,000
Commissions	= (250)
Net proceeds upon receipt of shares from conversion in about one month	= $15,750
Sell 400 shares and convert on June 1	
Sell 400 common stock at $40	= $16,000
Commissions	= (250)
Dividends paid at $.10 per share	= (40)
Bond interest received	= 500
Net proceeds upon receipt of shares from conversion in about two months	= $16,210

From the analysis, the normal choice would be to convert after June 1. The extra $394 earned ($16,210 − $15,816) on the position for less than two additional months equates to an annualized rate of return above 15 percent.

Note that the 400 share sale prior to receiving common stock upon conversion is technically treated as a *short* sale. Some investors will not sell stock short for any reason (some institutions are legally prevented from doing so). If you fit this prohibited category, rather than accept an abnormally low bid, ask your broker if his firm's arbitrage department would be willing to take the position into its inventory at a more favorable price. This question should be asked before opening an account since it is a close-out strategy that you will wish to employ frequently.

Responding to a Call Notice

The calculations of Table C–1 assume that the bond had not been called; thus interest would be received on June 1. Most companies will call in their convertible bonds when they trade well above par and the usual 30 day notice is frequently timed to fall just prior to the interest payment date. In the example, if the company issued a call notice on April 30, with a May 30 expiration date, bondholders would be forced to convert to obtain the 160 conversion value, but they would not receive any interest. The usual close out procedure is to short the stock and immediately issue conversion instructions to the brokerage firm holding the bonds.

Since most convertible bondholders do not intend to retain common stock received on the exchange, a call notice increases the supply of stock available for sale in the marketplace. Therefore, expect to see a stock price drop when a call notice is issued—the extent of the decline will depend on the bond's size and how active the stock trades. Expecting downward price pressure during the 30-day conversion period, alert bondholders will often sell stock short within minutes after the call notice is announced. Be aware that the short sale is exempt from the uptick rule, so a market order identified as *short exempt* may be executed, if desired.

Low-Risk Convertibles Purchased, 1976—June 1984

Company	Convertible Description	Purchase Data		Sale Data	
		Date	Price	Date	Price
Chase Manhattan	4.875–93	12–75	61.00	4–76	68.25
Federal Nat'l. Mtg.	4.375–96	12–75	77.75	1–76	82.00
Gulf & Western	5.50 –93	12–75	82.00	1–76	95.50
Tesoro Petroleum	5.25 –89	12–75	82.75	1–77	102.00
United Technologies	4.50 –92	12–75	66.50	4–76	88.25
International Tel. & Tel.	$ 2.25 pfd.	12–75	41.00	1–76	45.00
Greyhound	6.50 –90	1–76	82.25	8–76	90.75
Grace	6.50 –96	5–76	94.12	12–76	99.50
Federal Nat'l Mtg.	4.375–96	5–76	72.75	10–76	80.75
International Tel. & Tel.	$ 2.25 pfd.	6–76	31.25	8–76	38.62
Woolworth	$ 2.20 pfd.	7–76	35.00	12–76	37.50
Ford Motor	4.875–98	8–76	82.50	8–78	85.38
Gulf & Western	5.50 –93	10–76	90.75	4–77	78.25
National Distillers	4.50 –92	12–76	95.00	11–77	87.25
American Hoist	5.50 –93	12–76	89.00	5–77	123.00
Continental Telephone	5.25 –86	12–76	82.50	9–77	85.25
Beech Aircraft	4.75 –93	12–76	81.00	12–77	96.00
Airco	3.875–87	12–76	96.00	6–77	105.00
U. V. Industries	5.75 –93	12–76	81.25	8–78	94.71
North Amer. Philips	4.00 –92	12–76	77.44	6–77	77.39

Company	Convertible Description	Purchase Data Date	Purchase Data Price	Sale Data Date	Sale Data Price
Hilton Hotels	5.50 -95	12–76	85.50	6–77	87.00
Parker Hannifan	4.00 -92	12–76	74.62	6–77	87.00
Storer Broadcasting	4.50 -86	12–76	85.00	5–77	86.12
Federal Nat'l. Mtg.	4.375-96	12–76	85.75	8–78	99.00
GAF Corp.	$ 1.20 pfd.	12–76	18.58	2–77	18.69
White Consolidated	5.50 -93	1–77	101.50	6–77	106.50
City Investing	7.50 -90	1–77	99.50	6–77	104.75
Zapata	4.75 -88	2–77	77.91	7–77	70.94
Houston Industries	5.50 -85	2–77	94.50	10–80	80.50
Citicorp	5.75 -00	2–77	94.50	3–78	75.12
E-Systems	4.50 -92	2–77	86.25	11–77	84.00
Melville	4.875-96	2–77	89.00	4–78	94.00
Tesoro Petroleum	5.25 -89	2–77	94.00	9–77	80.00
Ogden	5.00 -93	3–77	71.00	1–78	69.00
Sola Basic	4.50 -92	3–77	90.12	5–77	120.00
Woolworth	$ 2.20 pfd.	4–77	34.50	11–77	30.00
Dayco	6.25 -96	5–77	93.00	7–79	100.00
Castle & Cooke	5.375-94	5–77	79.00	8–78	110.50
Harrah's	7.50 -96	6–77	111.50	5–78	147.00
Lear Siegler	$ 2.25 pfd.	6–77	41.00	2–78	37.75
Texasgulf Inc.	$ 3.00 pfd.	10–77	39.50	5–78	38.50
Hilton Hotels	5.50 -95	11–77	86.75	5–78	115.00
Pennwalt	$ 1.60 pfd.	11–77	23.50	7–78	24.38
Foremost McKesson	$ 1.80 pfd.	11–77	28.83	5–78	34.25
Amerada Hess	$ 3.50 pfd.	12–77	62.88	4–78	64.00
Gulf & Western	$ 2.50 pfd.	12–77	30.25	5–78	34.00
Beech Aircraft	4.75 -93	1–78	91.00	2–78	102.00
Chromalloy American	$ 5.00 pfd.	1–78	63.00	6–78	92.79
Carrier	$ 1.86 pfd.	2–78	27.75	4–78	34.50
Holiday Inns	$ 1.70 pfd.	2–78	24.50	4–78	26.22
Humana	6.00 -99	4–78	100.00	7–78	122.72
Textron	$ 1.40 pfd.	4–78	23.50	9–80	17.50
GAF Corp.	$ 1.20 pfd.	4–78	16.42	9–80	17.50
McDermott	$ 2.20 pfd.	4–78	31.88	9–78	33.00
White Consolidated	5.50 -92	5–78	90.50	6–78	91.00

Company	Convertible Description	Purchase Data Date	Purchase Data Price	Sale Data Date	Sale Data Price
Gulf & Western	5.50 –93	5–78	84.50	2–80	105.00
City Investing	7.50 –90	5–78	101.25	7–79	111.50
Wometco Enterprises	5.50 –94	6–78	96.00	8–78	111.00
Household Finance	$ 2.50 pfd.	6–78	32.50	6–80b	28.50
Zale	$ 0.80 pfd.	6–78	13.38	8–78	14.38
Storer Broadcasting	4.50 –86	7–78	90.55	4–79	111.50
Fruehauf	5.50 –94	7–78	76.50	6–79	83.00
Lone Star Industries	5.125–93	7–78	85.00	6–79	95.00
Carrier	$ 1.86 pfd.	7–78	33.75	12–78	50.21
Rockwell International	4.25 –91	8–78	78.48	3–79	80.75
Federal Nat'l. Mtg.	4.375–96	8–78	92.00	4–79	81.88
Host International	5.25 –94	8–78	76.25	9–78	79.00
Chromalloy American	$ 5.00 pfd.	8–78	77.25	3–79	76.33
Holiday Inns	$ 1.70 pfd.	8–78	30.38	12–78	29.62
Woolworth	$ 2.20 pfd.	8–78	30.00	4–79	42.00
Reserve Oil & Gas	$ 1.75 pfd.	8–78	23.88	3–79	24.88
U.S. Gypsum	$ 1.80 pfd.	8–78	29.50	8–79	32.00
Amfac	$ 1.00 pfd.	8–78	12.75	12–79	14.25
Grace (W. R.)	6.50 –92	9–78	96.50	11–78	100.50
Owens-Illinois	4.50 –92	9–78	84.62	12–78	69.50
Bally Manufacturing	6.00 –98	9–78	100.00	12–78	83.25
Amerada Hess	$ 3.50 pfd.	9–78	66.58	12–78	63.00
TRW Corp.	$ 4.50 pfd.	9–78	75.00	4–79	72.00
Brunswick	$ 2.40 pfd.	10–78	33.88	12–78	28.25
Travelers	$ 2.00 pfd.	11–78	35.25	1–79	39.50
I.U. International	$ 1.36 pfd.	11–78	14.00	4–79	14.88
Carrier	5.125–89	12–78	91.50	7–79	97.73
Textron	$ 2.08 pfd.	1–79	28.50	1–80	31.62
INA Corp.	$ 1.90 pfd.	1–79	22.75	9–80	31.25
Tandy	6.50 –03	2–79	104.00	4–79	98.00
Bally Manufacturing	6.00 –98	2–79	106.00	3–79	115.00
Amerada Hess	$ 3.50 pfd	2–79	57.50	2–79	62.00
Crocker National	$ 3.00 pfd.	2–79	41.50	12–79	43.00
Brunswick	$ 2.40 pfd.	2–79	28.50	5–81	34.75
Amax	$ 3.00 pfd.	3–79	46.75	6–79	54.00
Arvin Industries	$ 2.00 pfd.	3–79	25.00	4–81	25.78

Company	Convertible Description	Purchase Data Date	Purchase Data Price	Sale Data Date	Sale Data Price
International Tel. & Tel.	$ 4.00 pfd.	4–79	46.00	8–80	48.97
FMC Corp.	4.25 –92	5–79	73.50	9–79a	76.12
Burlington Northern	5.25 –92	5–79	89.00	6–79	105.00
Greyhound	6.50 –90	5–79	88.00	12–80	80.00
Washington National	$ 2.50 pfd.	5–79	38.50	9–79a	39.38
Armco Steel	$ 2.10 pfd.	5–79	27.25	10–79	31.12
Carter Hawley Hale	$ 2.00 pfd.	5–79	27.25	10–79	31.00
Pitney-Bowes	$ 2.12 pfd.	5–79	29.00	6–80	38.00
Woolworth	$ 2.20 pfd.	6–79	37.00	9–79a	40.50
Alum. Co. America	5.25 –91	7–79	95.25	2–80	112.00
Dayco	6.00 –94	7–79	79.50	7–80	68.12
Insilco	$ 1.25 pfd.	7–79	16.12	6–80b	17.00
Phillips-Van Heusen	5.25 –94	8–79	64.00	9–79a	62.00
BanCal Tri-State	6.50 –96	9–79b	81.25	6–80	99.12
Ford Motor	4.50 –96	9–79b	68.50	12–79	55.38
Lone Star Industries	5.125–93	9–79b	95.00	12–79	96.00
North Amer. Philips	4.00 –92	9–79b	70.00	11–80	75.93
McDonnell Douglas	4.75 –92	9–79b	91.00	11–79	95.00
Riegel Textile	5.00 –93	9–79b	70.50	3–80	72.75
Walter, Jim	5.75 –91	9–79b	87.50	1–80	81.75
SCM Corp.	5.50 –88	9–79b	80.50	1–80	73.50
Amerace	$ 2.60 pfd.	9–79b	43.25	10–79	44.25
Arcata	$ 2.16 pfd.	9–79b	28.75	4–80	28.75
GK Technologies	$ 1.94 pfd.	9–79b	27.25	11–79	28.38
RCA Corp.	$ 4.00 pfd.	9–79b	54.00	2–80	51.00
United Technologies	$ 7.32 pfd.	9–79b	111.00	12–79	114.00
Western Union	$ 4.90 pfd.	9–79b	54.00	6–80b	59.00
Ford Motor	4.875–98	12–79	58.88	5–80	53.25
Cooper Industries	$ 2.90 pfd.	12–79	37.25	6–80	41.25
Reynolds Metals	4.50 –91	1–80	71.92	6–80	69.00
Georgia Pacific	$ 2.24 pfd.	1–80	31.75	7–82	24.50
RCA Corp.	$ 2.125 pfd.	2–80	19.25	6–80	21.50
Gulf & Western	5.50 –93	4–80	87.50	6–80b	100.00
Federal Nat'l. Mtg.	4.375–96	4–80	73.50	5–80	86.00
Foremost McKesson	6.00 –94	4–80	75.00	5–80	88.00

Company	Convertible Description	*Purchase Data* Date	*Purchase Data* Price	*Sale Data* Date	*Sale Data* Price
McDonnell Douglas	4.75 –92	5–80	93.25	10–80	110.00
Bally Manufacturing	6.00 –98	5–80	95.00	7–80	107.00
Natomas	$ 4.00 pfd.	5–80	58.50	6–80	64.75
United Technologies		5–80	51.00	8–80	63.25
	$ 3.875 pfd.				
Crocker National	5.75 –96	6–80	70.00	12–80	85.00
Owens-Illinois	4.50 –92	6–80	82.00	2–81	96.00
FMC Corp.	4.24 –92	6–80c	66.50	12–80	75.25
Tyco Laboratories	5.875–91	6–80c	89.25	9–80	113.77
Walter, Jim	5.75 –91	6–80c	85.00	7–80	89.50
Phillips-Van Heusen	5.25 –94	6–80c	55.75	8–80	64.00
RCA Corp.	$ 4.00 pfd.	6–80	50.00	8–80	57.25
Washington	$ 2.50 pfd.	6–80c	37.00	8–80	42.97
Bendix	$ 4.04 pfd.	6–80c	41.00	8–80	44.75
Western Union	$ 4.60 pfd.	6–80c	51.75	9–80	59.88
I. C. Industries	$ 3.50 pfd.	7–80	40.94	8–80	46.12
Citicorp	5.75 –00	8–80	66.90	4–81	69.00
Gulf United	9.25 –05	8–80	100.25	4–81	98.75
RCA Corp.		9–80	22.88	10–80	24.00
	$ 2.125 pfd.				
Reynolds Metals	4.50 –91	10–80	71.25	9–81	66.00
Bally Manufacturing	6.00 –98	11–80	85.62	5–81	101.50
Wang Labs	9.00 –05	12–80	121.50	5–81	133.00
Household Finance	$ 2.50 pfd.	12–80	25.75	3–81	27.38
Signal Companies	5.50 –94	12–80	84.50	9–82	64.50
RCA Corp.		2–81	22.50	11–80	16.25
	$ 2.125 pfd.				
Walter, Jim	5.75 –91	3–81	74.00	8–81	73.50
Edwards, A. G.	10.50 –06	3–81	103.42	6–82d	94.38
Moog	9.875–06	4–81	116.00	11–82	84.00
Dean Witter Reynolds	10.00 –05	4–81	113.00	12–81	183.15
Storage Technology	10.25 –00	4–81	119.00	10–81	149.50
Trinity Industries	10.00 –06	5–81	100.50	5–82	71.00
Hutton, E. F.	9.50 –05	6–81	109.00	4–83	159.89
U.S. Air	8.25 –05	7–81	104.00	12–81c	80.00

Company	*Convertible Description*	*Purchase Data*		*Sale Data*	
		Date	*Price*	*Date*	*Price*
Tiger International	8.625–05	8–81	78.00	3–82	49.00
Hospital Corp. of Amer.	8.75 –06	9–81	102.00	9–82	114.50
Nat'l. Medical Enterpr.	9.00 –06	9–81	74.00	10–81	86.20
Holiday Inns	9.625–05	9–81	116.50	12–81c	138.00
Oak Industries	11.00 –00	9–81	110.00	10–81	135.00
Ralston Purina	5.75 –00	10–81	74.00	2–82	83.50
Merrill Lynch	9.25 –00	11–81	103.60	11–82	150.50
Allied Chemical	7.75– 00	11–81	84.00	9–82	74.00
RCA Corp.	$ 4.00 pfd.	11–81	40.44	2–82	44.00
Nat'l. Medical Enterpr.	9.00 –06	11–81	80.00	4–82	74.50
Reading & Bates	$ 2.125 pfd.	11–81	33.00	3–82	21.82
Ashland Oil	$ 3.96 pfd.	11–81	38.25	8–82	33.00
Motorola	9.125–01	12–81d	87.00	4–82	105.00
Hercules	6.50 –99	12–81d	73.00	1–82	73.16
MGIC	5.00 –93	12–81d	80.00	1–82	83.36
Inexco Oil	8.50 –00	12–81d	103.25	1–83	70.00
Budd Company	9.00 –05	1–82	112.50	2–82	123.40
Bally Manufacturing	6.00 –98	1–82	93.00	7–82	111.00
Research-Cottrell	10.50 –06	1–82	99.50	6–82d	86.00
General Dynamics	$ 4.25 pfd.	1–82	55.31	4–82	67.00
Storage Technology	9.00 –01	1–82	100.12	1–83	95.00
Alexander & Alexander	11.00 –07	1–82	86.00	4–82	90.25
Heublein	4.50 –97	2–82	58.25	8–82	81.50
Mapco	10.00 –05	2–82	85.15	8–82	86.08
Oak Industries	10.50 –02	2–82	102.00	10–82	75.00
Pogo Producing	8.00 –05	4–82	86.50	1–83	82.50
Amer. Medical Int'l.	9.50 –01	4–82	89.25	10–83	113.50
RCA Corp.	$ 4.00 pfd.	5–82	50.00	11–82	61.00
McDermott	$ 2.20 pfd.	5–82	25.00	11–82	23.50
Viacom Int'l.	$ 2.10 pfd.	5–82	31.67	6–82d	28.50
Toys R Us	9.25 –07	5–82	120.00	10–82	143.07
Lifemark	9.00 –05	6–82	114.50	6–82d	112.50
Mapco	10.00 –05	7–82	84.00	11–82	88.25
Lifemark	9.00 –05	8–82	104.50	8–82	115.50
Georgia Pacific	5.25 –96	8–82	64.00	10–82	83.00

Company	*Convertible Description*	*Purchase Data*		*Sale Data*	
		Date	*Price*	*Date*	*Price*
Bendix	$ 4.04 pfd.	9–82	43.81	9–82	47.23
General American Oil	8.50 –05	9–82	94.00	1–83	107.00
Bally Manufacturing	10.00 –06	9–82	97.75	2–83	99.25
Becton Dickinson	4.125–88	10–82	88.00	11–82	95.00
Storer Broadcasting	8.50 –05	10–82	87.00	12–82	96.00
Rowan Companies	$ 2.44 pfd.	11–82	30.00	1–83	36.12
Merrill Lynch	8.875–07	11–82	115.00	2–83	128.00
Viacom Int'l.	9.25 –07	11–82	112.00	3–83	116.00
Wang Labs	9.50 –05	11–82	116.00	3–83	139.75
Greyhound	6.50 –90	11–82	97.00	2–83	116.86
Paine Webber	8.00 –07	12–82	99.00		
Nat'l. Medical Enterpr.	9.00 –06	12–82	107.50	3–83	118.74
Comcast	12.00 –96	1–83	108.50	7–83	130.91
Community Psychiatric	11.00 –91	1–83	120.00	5–83	158.00
Becton Dickinson	4.125–88	1–83	92.00	5–83	100.50
Mapco	9.00 –03	2–83	99.00	4–83	107.13
Lifemark	11.00 –02	2–83	116.00	5–83	143.59
Storage Technology	9.00 –01	2–83	92.50	5–83	94.50
Bally Manufacturing	6.00 –98	2–83	90.00	9–83c	91.00
Walter, Jim	9.00 –07	3–83	111.00	5–83	124.57
Goodrich, B. F.	$ 3.125 pfd.	3–83	33.75	5–83	34.88
Rowan Companies	$ 2.44 pfd.	3–83	36.00	6–83	40.75
Nat'l. Medical Enterpr.	12.625–01	3–83	17.50		
Searle, G. D.	5.25 –89	4–83	90.00	8–83	117.00
Quaker State Oil	8.875–08	5–83	106.00		
MacMillan	8.75 –08	5–83	108.50	6–83	124.00
Data Design Labs	12.25 –00	5–83	130.50	12–83	125.00
Research-Cottrell	10.50 –06	5–83	115.00	1–84	106.20
CPT Corp.	10.00 –01	5–83	118.00	12–83	88.50
Comdisco	8.00 –03	5–83	102.00	1–84	62.75
Pogo Producing	8.00 –05	6–83	80.25		
Zenith Radio	8.375–05	7–83	128.50	8–83	147.85
Newell Companies	8.75 –03	8–83	92.00		
Leggett & Platt	8.125–01	9–83	111.50		
Allied Corp.	7.75 –05	9–83e	103.12		

Company	Convertible Description	Purchase Data		Sale Data	
		Date	*Price*	*Date*	*Price*
Allied Stores	9.50 –07	9–83e	132.00		
American Maize Products	11.75 –00	9–83e	113.00	12–83	111.88
American General	11.00 –07	9–83e	126.00		
Barnett Banks of Florida	12.25 –06	9–83e	137.50		
Celanese	9.75 –06	9–83e	113.50		
Chase Manhattan	6.50 –96	9–83e	84.00		
Conserv	11.00 –07	9–83e	80.00	12–83	62.00
Equitable Gas	9.50 –06	9–83e	125.25	3–84	139.00
GTE Corp.	10.50 –07	9–83e	114.00		
Lifemark	13.00 –01	9–83e	123.00		
Seagram Company	8.25 –08	9–83e	106.25		
United Telecommunications	5.00 –93	9–83e	82.12		
Walter, Jim	5.75 –91	9–83e	88.00		
Transtechnology	9.00 –03	9–83e	99.50	12–83	98.00
McKesson	9.75 –06	10–83	103.00		
Reynolds, R. J.	10.00 –08	10–83	112.25		
Merrill Lynch	8.875–07	10–83	128.50		
Moran Energy	8.75 –08	11–83	95.25		
Nat'l. Convenience Stores	9.00 –08	1–84	103.00		
Viacom International	9.25 –07	1–84	114.62		
Southwest Airlines	10.00 –07	4–84	124.00		
SCOA Industries	10.00 –07	4–84	102.55		
Inexco Oil	8.50 –00	4–84	83.45		
Burlington Industries	5.00 –91	5–84	80.38		

Note: This table presents convertibles purchased for the author's most diversified managed accounts beginning late 1975. Where an account was replaced by a new, more diversified account, end of the quarter prices were used to close out an older convertible not held by the new account or to establish starting prices for convertibles held by the new account not held by the former. These are shown by a, b, c, d or e for the five clients involved in the study.

Aggressive Convertibles Purchased, 1976—June 1984

Company	*Convertible Description*	*Purchase Data*		*Sale Data*	
		Date	*Price*	*Date*	*Price*
Pan American	7.50 -98	12-75	78.00	6-76	92.75
Occidental Petroleum	$ 3.60 pfd.	12-75	46.88	6-76	57.25
El Paso	6.00 -93	3-76	83.00	1-77	93.00
Avco	9.625-01	10-76	103.50	12-76	160.50
PanAmerican	7.50 -98	10-76	76.25	3-77	76.88
Riegel Textile	5.00 -93	12-76	77.50	6-78	80.00
Budd Company	5.875-94	12-76	91.88	1-78	142.00
Wallace Murray	6.50 -91	12-76	100.00	3-77	118.00
Grumman	4.25 -92	1-77	61.50	6-77	69.75
Oak Industries	4.375-87	5-77	70.00	6-77	72.00
Avco	9.625-01	6-77	114.50	7-78	160.50
Pan American	7.50 -98	6-77	88.50	9-78	120.00
Arvin Industries	$ 2.00 pfd.	6-77	28.00	5-78	33.40
Curtiss Wright	$ 2.00 pfd.	6-77	27.25	10-77	26.00
Grumman	8.00 -99	7-77	111.00	5-78	109.25
National City Lines	5.50 -88	10-77	70.00	7-78	60.00
Republic N.Y.	5.375-97	11-77	74.50	7-78	91.00
Cooper Laboratories	4.50 -92	12-77	66.50	9-79a	63.50
Kaiser Cement	$ 2.50 pfd.	1-78	34.62	8-78	50.00
Western Airlines	5.25 -93	4-78	80.00	6-78	104.00

Company	*Convertible Description*	*Purchase Data*		*Sale Data*	
		Date	*Price*	*Date*	*Price*
Allegheny Airlines	9.25 -99	5–78	131.00	6–78	182.00
Phoenix Steel	6.00 -87	6–78	84.00	3–79	70.00
TRE Corp.	9.75 -02	6–78	124.88	9–78	126.00
General Instrument	10.25 -96	6–78	124.50	8–78	132.75
Eastern Airlines	10.00 -02	6–78	123.50	8–78	137.00
Mohawk Data Sciences	12.00 -89	7–78	126.00	9–78	124.00
Litton Industries	3.50 -87	8–78	70.00	6–80b	115.00
Ramada Inns	10.00 -00	8–78	126.00	9–78	159.00
Kaiser Cement	$ 1.375 pfd.	8–78	19.50	8–79	22.50
McDonnell Douglas	4.75 -91	9–78	118.00	1–79	114.00
Pan American	9.875-96	10–78	117.00	12–78	122.50
Western Airlines	5.25 -93	11–78	84.00	7–79	95.00
Ramada Inns	10.00 -00	11–78	117.00	5–79	173.50
Di Giorgio	5.75 -93	11–78	74.50	1–79	82.00
El Paso	6.00 -93	12–78	90.25	2–79	102.00
Ltv Corp.	$ 2.60 pfd.	1–79	24.38	6–80	29.50
Punta Gorda Isles	$ 1.104 pfd.	4–79	11.75	9–79a	12.88
Texasgulf	$ 3.00 pfd.	5–79	41.50	10–79	50.25
Conn. General Mortgage	6.00 -96	8–79	81.00	10–80	93.00
Grumman	8.00 -99	9–79	102.00	1–80	142.00
NFC Corp.	8.00 -92	9–79b	93.50	11–80	122.75
Trans World	5.00 -94	9–79b	58.00	5–80	44.00
UAL Corp.	4.25 -92	10–79	55.00	10–81	40.00
Western Airlines	5.25 -93	11–79	75.00	12–79	93.00
Sherwin Williams	6.25 -95	12–79	71.00	5–80	73.00
Fairmont Foods	9.00 -96	12–79	94.62	6–80	106.00
Phoenix Steel	6.00 -87	2–80	65.00	5–80	65.00
National Kinney	5.25 -97	2–80	44.00	7–80	39.38
Sanders Associates	7.00 -92	3–80	76.50	5–80	82.50
Mattel	$ 2.50 pfd.	3–80	20.00	5–80	23.25
Ramada Inns	10.00 -00	4–80	109.50	6–81	141.90
Ozark Air Lines	5.25 -86	8–80	64.75	4–81	130.64
LTV Corp.	12.00 -05	6–80	101.50	2–81	198.35
Cooper Laboratories	4.50 -92	6–80c	64.75	12–80	84.60
Warnaco	$ 1.50 pfd.	6–80c	29.25	3–81	36.55
Grumman	11.00 -00	7–80	117.00	6–82d	123.75

Company	Convertible Description	Purchase Data Date	Purchase Data Price	Sale Data Date	Sale Data Price
Allegheny Ludlum	4.00 -81	7-80	95.80	7-80	100.00
American Airlines	5.25 -98	10-80	48.94	2-81	55.50
Zenith Radio	8.375-05	10-80	102.00	8-83	160.09
Energy Resources	9.00 -95	10-80	103.80	4-83	92.24
U.S. Realty Investment	5.75 -89	11-80	75.82	4-81	88.48
Ampex	5.50 -94	11-80	77.50	12-80	84.50
Western Union	$ 4.60 pfd.	11-80	56.25	10-81	58.04
Inexco Oil	8.50 -00	12-80	119.50	12-81c	103.25
Crystal Oil	11.375-00	1-81	112.58	3-81	150.00
Computer Sciences	6.00 -94	1-81	83.00	5-82	66.00
Prime Computer	10.00 -00	1-81	130.00	3-81	112.50
Macrodyne	12.50 -95	1-81	108.00	12-81c	82.00
Newbery Energy	12.00 -95	2-81	87.00	8-82	55.00
Columbia Pictures	8.25 -00	2-81	104.00	12-81c	113.12
Vishay Intertechnology	11.00 -00	2-81	88.00	7-83	134.14
Instrument Systems	12.00 -99	3-81	94.25	8-81	79.50
Eastern Airlines	11.75 -05	4-81	96.62	1-82	70.00
Recognition Equipment	11.00 -06	4-81	115.00	7-82	58.00
Transtechnolgy	12.50 -01	4-81	98.00	6-83	186.09
GAF Corp.	$ 1.20 pfd.	4-81	15.75	6-81	18.94
MGM Grand Hotels	9.50 -00	4-81	79.23	8-82	62.31
Energy Management	12.00 -96	5-81	104.00	6-82d	72.00
Sanders Associates	7.00 -92	5-81	107.00	12-82	104.60
Health Chem.	10.375-99	5-81	102.75	8-82	67.67
TIE Communications	11.50 -01	5-81	114.00	11-82	142.65
Punta Gorda Isles	6.00 -92	6-81	73.50	5-82	54.00
Fuqua Industries	5.75 -88	6-81	75.00	1-82	99.00
Trans World	12.00 -05	6-81	113.00	11-81	96.00
Prime Computer	10.00 -05	6-81	124.00	11-81	103.00
PSA Inc.	11.125-04	7-81	108.50	9-82	105.00
Ramada Inns	10.00 -00	7-81	108.50	5-83	138.25
Nat'l. Education	9.875-00	7-81	103.62	11-82	131.62
Tacoma Boatbuilding	10.75 -01	8-81	95.50	1-82	103.22
Fairfield Communities	9.75 -03	8-81	107.08	10-82	123.53
Crystal Oil	11.375-00	9-81	104.50		
Galaxy Oil	9.00 -94	10-81	100.00	12-81c	96.50

Company	Convertible Description	Purchase Data		Sale Data	
		Date	Price	Date	Price
Brunswick	10.00 –06	10–81	99.00	3–82	114.86
Pogo Producing	8.00 –05	10–81	82.00	12–81c	85.00
Four-Phase Systems	9.125–01	12–81	91.12	12–81c	87.00
Lynch Communications	8.50 –99	12–81d	70.00	6–82d	64.00
Zayre	5.75 –94	12–81d	72.00	4–82	78.00
U.S. Air	8.25 –05	12–81d	80.00	8–82	100.00
Williams Companies	11.00 –96	12–81d	97.25	4–83	98.50
Dorchester Gas	8.50 –05	4–82	70.68	6–82d	64.00
Trans World	12.00 –05	4–82	107.00	6–82d	105.00
Brunswick	10.00 –06	5–82	94.00	6–83	186.28
Mattel	$ 2.50 pfd.	5–82	35.75	10–82	45.00
Tiger International	8.625–05	3–82	49.00	11–82	52.00
Galaxy Oil	9.00 –94	6–82c	62.50	10–82	52.62
Anacomp	9.50 –00	7–82	94.25	12–82	117.50
Lynch Communications	8.50 –99	7–82	61.50	12–82	72.00
Trans World	5.00 –94	8–82	46.00	10–82	50.50
Dorchester Gas	8.50 –00	9–82	63.50	12–82c	66.00
Comdisco	13.00 –01	10–82	125.50	12–82	136.54
Beefsteak Charlies	13.00 –97	10–82	103.00		
U.S. Air	9.25 –07	10–82	106.00		
Financial Corp. of Amer.	11.50 –02	10–82	110.25	4–83	189.19
Rohr Industries	$ 3.125 pfd.	11–82	31.75	12–82c	31.00
Integrated Resources	$ 3.07 pfd.	11–82	31.25	12–82	38.50
Western Union	5.25 –97	11–82	78.75	12–82	78.10
Horn & Hardart	11.25 –00	11–82	112.50	12–82	117.50
NBI Communications	8.25 –07	12–82	101.75	12–82	104.33
Delmed	10.50 –02	12–82	101.75	12–82c	103.75
Anacomp	13.875–02	12–82e	117.50	3–83	146.96
Delmed	10.50 –02	12–82	101.75	12–82c	103.75
Anacomp	13.875–02	12–82e	117.50	3–83	146.96
Mobile Communications	12.00 –02	12–82e	148.00		
Tacoma Boatbuilding	10.75 –01	12–82e	136.00	2–83	145.43
Trans World	12.00 –05	12–82e	126.00	4–83	151.54
Athlone Industries	11.375–01	1–83	100.00	6–83	140.54
Western Air Lines	5.25 –93	2–83	69.00	6–83	73.15
Volt Info Sciences	12.125–01	3–83	124.00	6–83	134.97

Company	Convertible Description	Purchase Data Date	Purchase Data Price	Sale Data Date	Sale Data Price
Saveway Industries	9.75 –00	3–83	122.00	5–83	146.41
Mor-Flo Industries	14.00 –01	3–83	130.30	5–83	160.79
Delmed	10.50 –02	3–83	109.60	5–83	112.66
Southwest Forest Ind.	10.00 –03	3–83	98.00	3–84	137.50
PSA Inc.	11.125–04	4–83	118.75	5–84	99.36
Andersen Group	10.50 –02	4–83	120.00		
Gulfstream Land	14.375–01	5–83	128.25	7–83	143.61
MGM Grand	9.50 –00	5–83	86.00		
Inter-Regional	11.50 –02	5–83	120.00		
Recognition Equipment	11.00 –06	6–83	115.00		
Delmed	10.50 –02	6–83	115.36		
Crime Control	10.00 –97	6–83	112.00		
Computer Consoles	7.75 –98	6–83	118.00		
Punta Gorda Isles	6.00 –92	7–83	75.94	2–84	67.23
Eastern Air Lines	11.75 –05	7–83	101.43	9–73	88.78
Dorchester Gas	8.50 –05	7–83	78.75	2–84	78.00
Anacomp	13.875–02	7–83	112.92		
Bowmar Instruments	13.50 –95	7–83	116.72	2–84	94.58
Global Marine	18.00 –03	7–83	94.50	1–84	89.89
Singer Company	9.00 –02	7–83	99.00	11–83	96.00
Graphic Scanning	10.00 –01	8–83	100.00		
American Century	6.75 –91	8–83	83.00		
Prairie Producing	9.25 –03	9–83	117.65		
Brunswick	8.50 –98	10–83	125.00	12–83	140.11
Pan American	15.00 –98	10–83	133.81	1–84	163.64
Pulte Home	8.50 –08	11–83	111.40		
Lear Petroleum	9.00 –03	12–83	83.50	3–84	93.45
American Maize Products	11.75 –00	12–83	111.88		
CPT Corp.	10.00 –01	12–83	88.50		
Data-Design Labs	12.25 –00	12–83	125.00		
Comserv	11.00 –02	12–83	62.00		
Western Air Lines	14.00 –98	1–84	105.00		
Pan American	15.00 –98	2–84	134.09		
Koger Properties	9.25 –03	2–84	91.00		
American Adventure	10.00 –982	3–84	98.00		

Company	*Convertible Description*	*Purchase Data*		*Sale Data*	
		Date	*Price*	*Date*	*Price*
Carl Karcher Enterpr.	9.50 –07	3–84	111.00		
Telepictures	10.00 –02	5–84	107.50		
Lear Petroleum	9.00 –03	5–84	91.00		
Southwest Forest Ind.	10.00 –03	5–84	108.00		
Walker Telecommunications	11.00 –99	6–84	99.50		

Note: This table presents convertibles purchased for the author's most diversified managed accounts beginning late 1975. Where an account was replaced by a new, more diversified account, end of the quarter prices were used to close out an older convertible not held by the new account or to establish starting prices for convertibles held by the new account not held by the former. These are shown by a, b, c, d, or e for the five clients involved in the study.

Companies Having Actively Traded Convertible Bonds, Convertible Preferreds, or Warrants

Company	Convertible Bonds	Convertible Preferreds	Warrants
	Number of Issues—Market Value, $Million		
AMR Corp.		1– 163.8	
ARA Services	1– 8.4		
Acton Corp.			1– 0.9
Acapulco Restaurants	1– 9.1		
Advest Group	1– 21.2		
Alaska Airlines	1– 23.0		
Alco Standard	1– 50.0		
Alexanders	1– 15.1		
Allegheny International		1– 226.2	
Allied Corp.	1– 78.6	2– 364.2	
Allied Stores	1–139.8		
Allis-Chalmers		1– 38.44	

Company	Number of Issues—Market Value, $Million Convertible Bonds	Convertible Preferreds	Warrants
Amax Inc.		1– 9.3	
Amerace Corp.	1– 10.0	1– 28.0	
Amerada Hess		1– 61.1	
American Brands		1– 105.0	
American Can		1– 100.9	
American Century Corp.	1– 6.2		
American Express			1–56.0
American General	2–375.6	3–1225.9	1–70.0
American Hoist & Derrick	1– 66.5		
American Int'l. Group	1– 19.3	1– 107.0	
American-Maize Products	1– 26.2		
American Medical Int'l.	4–313.9		
American Motors	1– 15.9		
Amer. S & L Assn. of Fla.		1– 44.0	
American Water Works		1– 4.9	
Amfac Inc.	2– 29.1	1– 8.2	
Anacomp Inc.	1– 25.7		
Andersen Group	1– 9.2		
Angeles Corp.			1– 2.4
Anheuser-Busch		1– 363.8	
Anixter Brothers	1– 36.5		
Anthony Industries	1– 20.1		
Apache Petroleum			1–12.6
Armco Inc.		1– 41.2	
Arrow Electronics	1– 24.9		
Arvin Industries		1– 9.9	
Ashland Oil		1– 126.2	
Associated Dry Goods		1– 243.6	
Atlantic Research	1– 26.1		
Atlantic Richfield		2– 371.8	
Atlas Corp.			1– 4.0
Avco Corp.	1– 44.6	1– 94.4	
Aviation Group	1– 21.2		
Avnet Inc.	1– 88.5		
Bally Manufacturing	2–117.1		1– 6.4

Company	Convertible Bonds	Convertible Preferreds	Warrants
	Number of Issues—Market Value, $Million		
BancTEXAS Group		1– 8.4	
Bank New York	2–107.4		
BankAmerica Realty Inv.	2– 50.3		
Bard, C. R.	1– 19.2		
Barnett Banks Florida	1– 68.2	1– 87.0	
Baxter Travenol Labs	2– 95.8		
Bearings Inc.	1– 41.2		
Beatrice Companies		1– 185.4	
Becton Dickinson	3–373.8		
Beefsteak Charlies	1– 9.7		
Beker Industries			1– 3.5
Bell & Howell		1– 114.2	
Bethlehem Steel		2– 197.2	
Beverly Enterprises	1– 86.0		
Big Three Industries	1– 79.0		
Bio-Response Inc.			1– 4.5
Bird Inc.		1– 9.5	
Boeing Co.	1–297.4		
Boise Cascade		1– 94.0	
Bowmar Instrument	1– 9.2		
Bristol-Meyers Co.		1– 21.0	
Brown & Sharpe Mfg.	1– 13.6		
Burlington Industries	2– 74.0		
Burnup & Sims	1– 25.9		
CIGNA Corp.		1– 149.6	
CPT Corp.	1– 31.5		
CSX Corp.		1– 15.8	
Caesars World			1– 0.9
CalFed Inc.		1– 77.0	
Cannon Group	1– 30.6		
Canon Inc.	1– 35.5		
Carl Karcher Enterprises	1– 24.1		
Castle & Cooke	1– 16.1	1– 10.8	
Caterpillar Tractor	1–111.4		
Ceco Corp.	1– 10.1		

	Number of Issues—Market Value, $Million		
Company	*Convertible Bonds*	*Convertible Preferreds*	*Warrants*
Celanese Corp.	2–124.7		
Cessna Aircraft	1– 79.5		
Champion International		2– 155.9	
Chapman Energy		1– 9.6	
Charter Co.		1– 3.0	1– 1.7
Chase Manhattan	2– 71.6		
Chemical New York	2– 29.8	1– 38.9	
ChemLawn Corp.	1– 14.7		
Chris Craft Industries		1– 84.6	
Chromalloy American		1– 40.0	
Cincinnati Financial	1– 29.6		
Circle K Corp.	1– 58.1		
Citicorp	1– 21.2		
City Federal S & L		2– 90.0	
City Investing	1– 8.2	2– 398.6	
Clevepak Corp.		1– 43.7	
Cluett Peabody & Co.		1– 24.1	
Coastal Corp.		1– 11.2	
Codenoll Technology			1– 2.8
Collins Foods			1– 3.7
Commonwealth Edison		1– 18.2	
Communication Corp. America	1– 13.0		
Computer Consoles	1– 81.6		
Computer Horizons			1– 0.8
Computer Sciences	1– 28.0		
Comserv. Corp.	1– 8.0		
Comtech Inc.			1– 0.6
ConAgra Inc.		1– 28.7	
Conductron Corp.	1– 8.1		
Consolidated Edison		1– 27.9	
Consolidated Oil & Gas	2– 8.7		
Consul Corp.	1– 22.1		
Continental Group		1– 162.2	
Continental Telecom.	1– 3.6		
Cooper Industries		1– 169.9	

Company	Number of Issues—Market Value, $Million: Convertible Bonds	Convertible Preferreds	Warrants
Copperweld Corp.		1– 25.5	
Crime Control	1– 18.8		
Crocker National	1– 2.6	1– 17.0	
Crown Central Petroleum		1– 13.4	
Crown Zellerbach	1– 17.2	2– 164.6	
Crystal Oil	1– 38.5		
Custom Energy Services	1– 7.4		
DWG Corp.	1– 5.3		
Damson Oil			1– 1.0
Dana Corp.	1– 45.4		
Data-Design Labs	1– 23.8		
Datapoint Corp.	1– 63.1		
Dayco Corp.	2– 40.9		
Deere & Co.	2–208.2		
Delmed Inc.	1– 17.2		
Delta Air Lines	1– 9.6		
Denny's Inc.	1– 56.6		
Detroit Edison		1– 12.2	
Di Giorgio Corp.	2– 25.5	1– 9.4	
Diagnostic/Retrieval	1– 18.6		
Diamond Shamrock		1– 89.7	
Digicon Inc.	1– 14.1		1– 1.2
Digital Switch	1– 79.2		
Diversified Industries			1– 0.7
Dorchester Gas	1– 35.8		
Dreyfus Corp.	1– 66.8		
Eastern Air Lines	4–136.4	1– 25.0	3–14.0
Eastern Gas & Fuel	1– 46.8		
Eastman Kodak	1–255.7		
Eaton Corp.	1– 66.8		
Economics Labs	1– 13.6		
Electronic Memories & Mag.		1– 8.9	1– 2.5
Emerson Electric	1– 9.4		
Energy Factors	1– 28.1		
ENSERCH Corp.	1– 11.5		

Company	Number of Issues—Market Value, $Million Convertible Bonds	Convertible Preferreds	Warrants
ENSTAR Corp.		1– 155.0	
Equimark Corp.		1– 10.8	
Equitable Gas	1– 67.0		
Esmark Inc.		1– 108.6	
FMC Corp.	1– 44.6	1– 67.0	
FMI Financial			1–10.0
Fairchild Industries		1– 126.2	
Farah Manufacturing	1– 4.7		
Fedders Corp.	1– 6.0		
Federal Nat'l. Mortgage	1– 22.0		
Fidelcor Inc.		1– 63.5	
Figgie International	1– 9.9	1– 8.0	
Financial Corp. America	1– 44.6		
First Bank System	1– 28.0		
First Interstate Bancorp	1– 44.4	1– 107.5	
First Jersey National		1– 37.3	
First Nat'l. State Bancorp		1– 55.2	
First Pennsylvania Corp.	1– 36.0	1– 143.0	
First Security	1– 37.2		
First Union RE	1– 39.5		
Fischbach Corp.	2– 27.0		
Fisher Foods	1– 6.2		
Fleet Financial Group	1– 35.4		
Fleming Cos.	1– 51.2		
Flexi-Van Corp.	1– 9.9		
Foothill Group	1– 13.9		
Ford Motor	2–148.8		
Forum Group	1– 11.5		1– 1.4
Fourth Financial	1– 21.6		
Frontier Holdings	2– 32.3		1– 3.0
Fruehauf Corp.	1– 39.5	1– 42.9	
Fuqua Industries		1– 10.1	1–18.7
GAF Corp.		1– 57.2	
GATX Corp.	1– 29.1	1– 7.5	
GTE Corp.	4–333.6	1– 7.7	

	Number of Issues—Market Value, $Million		
Company	*Convertible Bonds*	*Convertible Preferreds*	*Warrants*
GTI Corp.			1- 0.9
Gelco Corp.	1- 67.1		
GenCorp Inc.			1- 5.3
General Growth Properties		1- 42.3	1-13.8
General Instrument	1- 7.7		
Genesco			1- 2.5
Genetic Engineering			1- 0.5
Genstar Corp.		1- 3.6	
Georgia Pacific	1- 83.1	2- 172.5	
Gibraltar Financial	1- 46.0		
Global Marine	1-102.6	1- 100.6	
Golden Nugget			1-52.5
Goulds Pumps	1- 22.8		
Grace (W. R.) & Co.	2- 27.1		
Grant Industries			1- 0.8
Graphic Scanning	1- 70.4		
Great Northern Nekoosa		1- 44.6	
Great Western Financial	1- 80.0		
Greatwest Hospitals	1- 29.6		
Greyhound Corp.	2- 31.3		
Grolier Inc.			1- 3.1
Gulf Resources & Chemical		1- 10.8	
HPSC Inc.		1- 10.8	
			1- 4.4
Hammermill Paper	1- 24.8		
Harnischfeger Corp.			1- 8.3
Hartmarx Corp.	1- 45.7		
Health-Chem Corp.	1- 15.2		
Heinz H. J. & Co.		1- 16.2	
Hercules Inc.	1- 46.5		
Hesston Corp.		1- 4.7	
Hitachi Ltd.	1-156.6		
Holiday Inns		1- 26.6	
Horn & Hardart			1-11.1

Company	*Number of Issues—Market Value, $Million* Convertible Bonds	Convertible Preferreds	Warrants
Hospital Corp. America	2–250.6		
Household International		3– 283.1	
Houston Industries	1– 35.4		
Hubbell Harvey Inc.		1– 43.2	
Hughes Tool Co.	1– 77.5		
IC Industries		1– 147.1	
ITT Corp.	1– 16.5	6– 413.6	
INCO Ltd.			1– 6.2
Inexco Oil	1– 44.8		
Ingersoll Rand		1– 72.1	
Inland Steel		1– 62.2	
Instrument Systems	1– 25.0	1– 3.9	1– 1.8
Integrated Resources		2– 196.1	
Inter-Regional Financial	2– 34.8		
INTERCO Inc.		1– 78.1	
InterFirst Corp.	1– 60.0		
International Banknote			1–10.0
International Harvester		1– 85.5	1–48.8
Int'l. Lease Finance	1– 26.0		
InterNorth		1– 312.9	
Interstate Bakeries	1– 11.5		
IPCO Corp.	1– 2.0		
Jamesway Corp.	1– 20.4		
Jerrico Corp.	1– 33.2		
Jet America Airlines	1– 9.9		
Jewel Cos.		1– 197.5	
K mart	1–189.3		
Kaiser Cement	1– 27.0	1– 11.5	
Kaneb Services	1– 35.6		
Katy Industries		1– 76.5	
Kaufman & Broad		2– 61.4	
Kelly-Johnston	1– 10.8		
Kerr Glass Manufacturing		1– 10.5	
Keystone International	1– 18.8		
Kidde Inc.		3– 56.2	1–11.2

Company	Number of Issues—Market Value, $Million		
	Convertible Bonds	*Convertible Preferreds*	*Warrants*
Kinder-Care Learning Center	1– 84.0		
Knoll International	1– 27.0		
Koger Properties	1– 17.4		
Kollmorgen	1– 38.6		
Komatsu Ltd.	1– 7.2		
Koppers Co.		1– 69.3	
Kulicke and Soffa	1– 38.1		
LTV Corp.		4– 335.4	
La Quinta Motor Inns	1– 24.2		
Lefarge Corp.		1– 30.8	
Lear Petroleum	1– 39.2	1– 53.6	
Lear Siegler Inc.		1– 27.5	
Leggett & Platt	1– 19.0		
Leisure + Technology	1– 21.2		
Libbney-Owens-Ford Co.		1– 72.4	
LIN Broadcasting	1–117.5		
Lincoln National Corp.		1– 40.6	
Lomas & Nettleton Financial	2–121.2		
Lone Star Industries		1– 58.1	
Lorimar	1– 10.1		
Lynch Commun. Systems	1– 9.1		
M/A-COM Inc.	1– 67.6		
MCI Communications	1–242.0		1–47.2
M.D.C. Corp.			1–11.2
MGM Grand Hotels	1– 33.0		
MGM/UA Entertainment			1–13.4
Macmillan Inc.	2– 63.2		
Macrodyne Industries	1– 7.8		
MAPCO Inc.	1– 96.4		
Mark Controls Corp.		1– 17.4	
Martin Marietta		1– 158.2	
MassMutual Mtg. & Realty	1– 5.6		
Mattel Inc.		1– 46.0	1–14.2
McDermott International		1– 74.9	1–52.5
McDonnell Douglas Corp.	1– 13.5		

	Number of Issues—Market Value, $Million		
Company	*Convertible Bonds*	*Convertible Preferreds*	*Warrants*
McGraw Hill Inc.	1– 3.6		
McKesson Corp.	2– 80.8	1– 20.1	
McLean Industries			1–39.0
MEDIQ Inc.	1– 29.1		
Melville Corp.	1– 12.0		
Mercantile Texas		1– 36.0	
Merrill Lynch & Co.	1–101.6		
MidCon Corp.	1– 98.5		
Mobile Corp.	1–216.9		
Mobile Commun. Corp. Amer.	1– 15.1		
Moog Inc.	1– 21.5		
Moore McCormack		1– 29.4	
Morgan J. P. Co.	1–101.6		
Muse Air			1– 1.2
NAFCO Financial Group	1– 16.8		
NBD Bancorp	1– 2.0		
NBI Inc.	1– 31.8		
NCNB Corp.			1– 8.9
Nat'l. Bankshares Texas	1– 25.2		
National Can Corp.		1– 10.9	
National Computer Systems	1– 10.6		
Nat'l. Convenience Stores	1– 44.0		
National Health Corp.	1– 22.3		
National Intergroup		1– 141.6	
Nat'l. Medical Enterprise	3–380.5		
Naugles Inc.			1– 2.2
New Plan Realty Trust	1– 31.5		
Newell Cos.	1– 24.0		
New York Air			1– 0.8
Newpark Resources			2– 0.8
Nortek Inc.			1– 2.6
Northview Corp.			1– 3.0
Northwest Airlines	1– 93.0		
Northwest Natural Gas		2– 13.4	
Norton Co.	1– 54.0		

Company	Convertible Bonds	Convertible Preferreds	Warrants
	Number of Issues—Market Value, $Million		
Norwest Corp.	1– 37.7		
Oak Industries	1– 54.5		
Occidental Petroleum		3– 41.2	
Offshore Logistics		2– 18.0	
Ogden Corp.	1– 9.7	1– 18.3	
Ohio Edison		1– 19.5	
Olin Corp.	1– 90.0		
Orion Pictures		1– 6.9	1– 6.8
Owens-Corning	1– 86.1		
Owens-Illinois	1– 17.3	1– 19.7	
OXOCO Inc.		1– 15.9	1– 1.9
PNC Financial	1– 49.5		
PSA Inc.	1– 27.5	1– 38.4	
Pacific Resources		1– 27.2	
Pacific Scientific	1– 18.6		
Paine Webber	2–137.7		
Pan American World Airways	3–228.7		1–28.8
Parker-Hannifin Corp.	1– 16.6		
Penn Central		1– 754.3	
Pennsylvania REIT	1– 38.1		
Pennwalt Corp.		1– 42.8	
Penril Corp.			1– 4.4
People Express Airlines		1– 62.1	
Perry Drug Stores	1– 12.4		
Petro-Lewis Corp.		1– 70.4	1– 4.8
Petroleum & Resources		1– 29.3	
Pfizer Inc.	2–202.8		
Phelps Dodge Corp.		1– 95.7	
Philips Industries Inc.		1– 8.3	
Piedmont Aviation	2–106.3		
Pier 1. Imports			1– 4.7
Pillsbury Co.	1– 2.5		
Pioneer-Standard Elec.	1– 22.6		
Pitney-Bowes Inc.		1– 154.1	
Pittston Co.	1– 19.7		

Company	*Number of Issues—Market Value, $Million* Convertible Bonds	Convertible Preferreds	Warrants
Pizza Inn	1– 8.5		
Pogo Producing	1– 43.5		
Prairie Producing	1– 27.9		
Production Operators	1– 17.1		
Property Capital Trust	1– 40.0		
Protective Corp.	1– 30.8		
Pulte Home	1– 44.4		
Punta Gorda Isles	1– 7.7		
Quaker State Oil	1– 48.0		
RCA Corp.	1– 79.3	2– 354.3	
Ralston Purina	1– 49.5		
Ramada Inns	1– 4.5		
Reading & Bates		1– 40.2	
Realty Income Trust	1– 10.3		
Recognition Equipment	1– 19.0		
Republic Airlines	1– 47.2		1– 4.7
RepublicBank Corp.		1– 41.0	
Research-Cottrell	1– 28.2		
Resorts International			1– 1.1
Rexnord Inc.	1– 47.5		
Reynolds R. J.	3–189.4		
Reynolds Metals Co.	1– 20.4	1– 18.2	
Riegel Textile Corp.	1– 7.1		
Rockaway Corp.	1– 13.4		
Rockwell International	1– 5.6	1– 52.1	
Rohr Industries	1– 32.8		
Ryan Homes	1– 5.2		
Rykoff S. E. & Co.	1– 22.3		
SCM Corp.	1– 21.6		
SRI Corp.	1– 23.2		
Safeguard Scientifics			1– 2.6
Sage Energy	1– 20.5		
St. Regis		1– 123.9	
Savin Corp.		1– 6.6	
Scientific Leasing	1– 22.0		

Company	Number of Issues—Market Value, $Million		
	Convertible Bonds	*Convertible Preferreds*	*Warrants*
SCOA Industries	1– 56.9		
Seagram Co.	1–127.2		
Searle G. D. & Co.	2– 31.3		
Service Merchandise	1– 56.7		
Sheller-Globe	1– 29.2	1– 3.6	
Sherwin-Williams	1– 13.8		
Signal Companies	1– 40.3	2– 136.0	
Singer Co.	1–100.0		
Southeast Banking Corp.	1– 11.2		
Southern Bancorp	1– 21.2		
Southern Calif. Edison		1– 7.0	
Southwest Airlines	1– 42.2		
Southwest Forest Industries	1– 47.7		
Sparkman Energy Corp.		1– 4.5	
Square D		1– 4.0	
Standard Havens			1– 2.2
Stanwood Corp.	1– 4.0		
State Street Boston	1– 45.5		
Stevens J. P.	1– 65.2		
Sterling Bancorp	1– 10.1		
Stop & Shop Companies	1– 89.9		
Storage Technology	1– 51.0		
Storer Communications	1–112.0		1–35.6
Summit Energy		1– 8.6	
Sun Co.		1– 122.5	
Sybrom Corp.		1– 20.7	
Symbol Technologies			1– 2.6
Syntex Corp.		1– 3.1	
TRE Corp.	1– 2.9		
TRW Inc.		2– 102.9	
Tacoma Boatbuilding	1– 10.3		
Talley Industries		1– 30.4	
Tele-Communications			1–33.1
Telepictures Corp.	1– 17.7		1– 4.2
Tesoro Petroleum Corp.	1– 3.4	1– 39.1	

Company	*Number of Issues—Market Value, $Million* Convertible Bonds	Convertible Preferreds	Warrants
Texas Air Corp.	2– 8.2	1– 28.4	
Texas Industries	1– 45.5		
Texfi Industries	1– 8.2		
Texas International			1– 0.6
Texscan Corp.	1– 27.2		
Textron Inc.		2– 67.2	
Thermo Electron	1– 26.1		
Tidewater Inc.	1– 34.0		
Tiger International			1– 6.3
Time Inc.		1– 180.0	
Timeplex	1– 28.1		
Total Petroleum			1– 2.5
Towle Manufacturing	1– 22.9		
Towner Petroleum			1– 0.3
Tracor Inc.	1– 47.5		
Trans World Airlines		1– 75.0	
Transco Energy Co.		1– 98.5	
TransTechnology	1– 14.1		
Transworld Corp.		2– 151.8	2–53.0
Trinity Industries	1– 55.5		
Triton Energy		1– 21.1	
Tyler Corp.			1–11.2
UAL Inc.		1– 261.3	
URS Corp.	1– 20.0		
Unifi Inc.			1– 5.2
Union Carbide	1–151.5		
Union Pacific Corp.	1– 16.6	1– 394.8	
Uniroyal Inc.	1– 42.3		
United Bancorp Arizona	1– 22.2		
United Banks Colorado	1– 19.9		
United Brands	1– 57.1	1– 19.8	
USAir Group	1–111.5		1– 5.6
United States Gypsum		1– 16.7	
U.S. Leasing International	1– 28.1		
U.S. Playing Card			1–11.0

Company	Convertible Bonds	Convertible Preferreds	Warrants
	Number of Issues—Market Value, $Million		
United States Steel	1–148.7	2– 663.3	
United Technologies		1– 635.9	
United Telecommunications	1– 12.3	1– 24.3	
Unitrode Corp.	1– 91.0		
Universal Health Services	1– 75.9		
USLIFE Corp.		1– 54.9	
Varco International		1– 6.4	
Viacom International	1– 63.0		
VICORP Restaurants	1– 45.5		
Victoria Bankshares	1– 14.6		
Wachovia Corp.		1– 20.2	
Wal-Mart Stores		1– 13.1	
Walter Jim Corp.	1–117.0	1– 18.6	
Wang Labs	2–246.4		
Warner Communications			1– 8.2
Washington National		1– 7.4	
Wayne Gossard Corp.		1– 7.1	
Weatherford		1– 18.2	
Webb Del E. Corp.			1– 1.8
Wells Fargo Mortgage	1– 29.0		
West Point-Pepperell	1– 5.0		
Western Air Lines	2– 69.0	2– 22.4	1– 8.5
Western Union Corp.	1– 32.4	1– 9.0	
Weyerhaeuser Co.		2– 294.1	
Williams Electronics	1– 15.0		
Wilson H J Co.	1– 18.0		
Winners Corp.	1– 19.6		
Witco Chemical Corp.	1– 6.1		
Woolworth F W Co.		1– 27.6	
Worldwide Energy		1– 15.0	
Wyle Laboratories	1– 5.8		
Xerox	1– 89.4		
Zurn Industries	1– 8.4		
Number of issues	358	216	84
Total market value, $mil	15,688	16,845	857

Source: *Value Line Convertibles*, July 9, 1984. Copyright 1984, Value Line, Inc. Consult this service or other sources for specific information on available convertibles and warrants.

Terms Applying to Convertibles and Warrants

Accrued interest. Interest earned on a bond since its last interest payment date. The buyer of the bond pays the market price plus accrued interest to the seller and is entitled to the next interest payment in full. Exceptions include bonds in default and income bonds, which are traded flat (without accrued interest).

Antidilution clause. Provisions contained in most convertible indentures calling for adjustment of the conversion terms in the event of stock splits, stock dividends, or the sale of new stock at a price below the conversion price of existing convertibles. In some cases, no adjustment is made for small stock dividends (e.g. under five percent in any single year or ten percent during the life of the convertible).

Arbitrage. See "Convertible arbitrage."

Beta. A tool which measures the historical sensitivity of a stock's price movements to overall market fluctuations, useful in identifying market risk.

Bond indenture. The contract under which bonds are issued. It describes such terms of the agreement as interest rate, interest payment dates, date of maturity, redemption terms, conversion privileges, antidilution clauses, and the security for the loan.

Bond price quotation. Bonds are quoted as a percentage of par. Thus, 90 represents 90 percent of a $1,000 bond, or $900. 110 means 110 percent of par, or $1,100.

Break-even time. The time period necessary for a convertible bond or convertible preferred to recapture the premium paid over conversion value, via the extra income, when bond interest or preferred dividends exceed the common stock's dividend.

Call price. The amount of money a corporation is obliged to pay if it chooses to redeem its senior securities. In the case of bonds, the call price is usually expressed as a percentage of par. In the case of preferred stock, the call is the price per share. The call price is normally set somewhat above par and is reduced periodically.

Callable. Term applying to securities whose indenture contains a provision giving the issuer the right to retire the issue prior to its maturity date.

Conversion parity. The price at which the convertible must sell for it to equal the current market value of the common shares to be received upon conversion. If the convertible is trading at a premium above conversion parity, it is generally better to sell the convertible rather than to convert.

Conversion premium. The difference between a convertible's market price and its conversion value expressed as a percentage above conversion value.

Conversion price. The price at which the underlying common stock must trade in order for the bond to be worth par value if converted.

Conversion ratio. The number of common shares to be received upon conversion.

Conversion value. The worth of a convertible bond or preferred if it is converted into common stock. It is calculated by multiplying the number of shares to be received upon conversion by the current market price of the common.

Convertible arbitrage. A simultaneous purchase and sale of related securities for an immediate profit upon conversion. This technique generally involves the purchase of a convertible bond or convertible preferred that is trading at a price below its conversion value, and the short sale of its common stock. The stock received from the conversion offsets the short sale.

Convertible bond. A debt instrument exchangeable at the option of the holder into common stock or other securities in accordance with the terms of the bond indenture.

Convertible preferred stock. An equity security, senior to the common stock, which may be exchanged at the option of the holder into common stock or other securities.

Convertible price curve. A graph showing the expected convertible price for any stock price over the near-term future.

Convertible strategies line. A graphical representation of risk-reward relationships for various investment strategies involving undervalued convertible securities.

Cumulative preferred. A preferred stock which provides for payment of its omitted dividends (arrearages) before dividends may be paid on the company's common stock.

Current yield. The interest or dividends paid annually by a company on a security, expressed as a percentage of the current market price of the security.

Default. Failure of the bond issuer to meet a contractual obligation, such as payment of interest, maintenance of working capital requirements, or payment of principal via a sinking fund or at maturity.

Discounted bond. A bond selling below par value.

Ex-dividend. A preferred or common stock trading without its current dividend. A seller of the security on the ex-dividend date will receive the dividend.

Expiration of conversion privileges. Termination date of a convertible's conversion privilege.

Fabricated convertible. A combination of warrants plus bonds usable for exercise purposes at par value in lieu of cash.

Forced conversion. Holders of convertibles may be forced to convert in order to capture conversion value if convertibles are called for redemption, if there is an adverse change in their conversion terms, or as an expiration date comes due.

Investment floor. See "Investment value."

Investment value. The estimated value of a convertible bond or convertible preferred stock without consideration of its conversion privilege. Also known as the investment floor.

Investment value premium. The difference between a convertible's market price and its investment value expressed as a percentage above investment value.

Maturity date. A fixed date when the company must redeem a bond by payment of the full face value to the bondholder.

Premium over conversion value. See "Conversion premium."

Premium over investment value. See "Investment value premium."

Profit profile. A graphic presentation of a risk-reward analysis which permits a visual comparison of investment alternatives.

Redemption. The act of retiring part or all of a bond issue prior to its maturity date. If a convertible bond issue is selling above the redemption price when it is called by the issuing company, redemption is equivalent to a forced conversion of the issue.

Registered bond. A bond which is issued in the name of the holder. Interest is paid by check to the holder. Most convertible bonds are registered.

Risk-reward analysis. A mathematical evaluation of a convertible relative to an appropriate combination of common stock and straight bonds used to identify undervalued investment alternatives.

Sinking fund provisions. A requirement calling for the company to begin retiring a convertible issue prior to its maturity date.

Subordinated debenture. A bond which is subject to the prior claim of other senior securities and usually not secured by any specific property.

Synthetic convertible. Created by an investment in both warrants and money market instruments.

Undervalued convertible. A convertible security having superior risk-reward characteristics relative to common stock and straight bonds, as determined by a risk-reward analysis.

Warrant. A negotiable security issued by a company which represents a long-term option to purchase common stock from the company on specified terms.

Warrant agreement. The contract under which warrants are issued.

Yield advantage. The difference between the yield of a convertible and its underlying common stock.

Yield to maturity. The effective yield of a bond, taking into account its premium or discount from par, if one holds it to maturity when it is expected to be redeemed by the company at par value.

INDEX

Probus Publishing Company Presents

Titles in Investment/ Personal Finance

The Investor's Equation: Creating Wealth Through Undervalued Stocks, by William M. Bowen IV and Frank P. Ganucheau III. ISBN 0-917253-00-0.

Stock Index Options: Powerful New Tools for Investing, Hedging, and Speculating, by Donald T. Mesler. ISBN 0-917253-02-7.

Winning the Interest Rate Game: A Guide to Debt Options, by Frank J. Fabozzi. ISBN 0-917253-01-9.

Maximize Your Gains: Tax Strategies for Today's Investor, by Robert W. Richards. ISBN 0-917253-10-8.

Increasing Your Wealth in Good Times and Bad, by Eugene M. Lerner and Richard M. Koff. ISBN 0-917253-06-X.

The Insider's Edge: Maximizing Investment Profits Through Managed Futures Accounts, by Bertram Schuster and Howard Abell. ISBN 0-917253-12-4.

The Handbook of Mortgage-Backed Securities, Frank J. Fabozzi, editor. ISBN 0-917253-04-3.

Personal Economics: A Guide to Financial Health and Well-Being, by Robert A. Kennedy and Timothy J. Watts. ISBN 0-917253-08-6.

Titles in Business

Revitalizing Your Business: Five Steps to Successfully Turning Around Your Company, by Edmund P. Freiermuth. ISBN 0-917253-05-1.

Compensating Yourself: Personal Income, Benefits and Tax Strategies for Business Owners, by Gerald I. Kalish. ISBN 0-917253-07-8.

Using Consultants: A Consumer's Guide for Managers, by Thomas A. Easton and Ralph Conant. ISBN 0-917253-03-5.

For further information, call Probus Publishing Company at (312) 346-7985.